CHRISTIAN HEROES: THEN & NOW

RACHEL SAINT

A Star in the Jungle

CHRISTIAN HEROES: THEN & NOW

RACHEL SAINT

A Star in the Jungle

JANET & GEOFF BENGE

YWAM PUBLISHING
P.O. BOX 55787 SEATTLE, WA 98155

YWAM Publishing is the publishing ministry of Youth With A Mission (YWAM), an international missionary organization of Christians from many denominations dedicated to presenting Jesus Christ to this generation. To this end, YWAM has focused its efforts in three main areas: (1) training and equipping believers for their part in fulfilling the Great Commission (Matthew 28:19), (2) personal evangelism, and (3) mercy ministry (medical and relief work).

For a free catalog of books and materials, call (425) 771-1153 or (800) 922-2143. Visit us online at www.ywampublishing.com.

Library of Congress Cataloging-in-Publication Data
Benge, Janet, 1958–
Rachel Saint : a star in the jungle / Janet and Geoff Benge.
p. cm. — (Christian heroes, then & now)
Includes bibliographical references.
ISBN 1-57658-337-6
1. Saint, Rachel—Juvenile literature. 2. Missionaries—Ecuador—Biography—Juvenile literature. 3. Missionaries—United States—Biography—Juvenile literature. I. Benge, Geoff, 1954– II. Title. III. Series.
BV2853.E3S345 2005
266'.0092—dc22

2005016786

Rachel Saint: A Star in the Jungle

Published by YWAM Publishing
a ministry of Youth With A Mission
P.O. Box 55787, Seattle, WA 98155

ISBN 978-1-57658-337-1 (paperback)
ISBN 978-1-57658-605-1 (e-book)

Fifth printing 2022

Printed in the United States of America

Christian Heroes: Then & Now

Adoniram Judson
Albert Schweitzer
Amy Carmichael
Betty Greene
Brother Andrew
Cameron Townsend
Charles Mulli
Clarence Jones
Corrie ten Boom
Count Zinzendorf
C. S. Lewis
C. T. Studd
David Bussau
David Livingstone
Dietrich Bonhoeffer
D. L. Moody
Elisabeth Elliot
Eric Liddell
Florence Young
Francis Asbury
George Müller
Gladys Aylward
Helen Roseveare
Hudson Taylor
Ida Scudder
Isobel Kuhn
Jacob DeShazer
Jim Elliot
John Flynn
John Newton
John Wesley
John Williams
Jonathan Goforth
Klaus-Dieter John
Lillian Trasher
Loren Cunningham
Lottie Moon
Mary Slessor
Mildred Cable
Nate Saint
Norman Grubb
Paul Brand
Rachel Saint
Richard Wurmbrand
Rowland Bingham
Samuel Zwemer
Sundar Singh
Wilfred Grenfell
William Booth
William Carey

Available in paperback, e-book, and audiobook formats.Unit study curriculum guides are available for select biographies.

www.YWAMpublishing.com

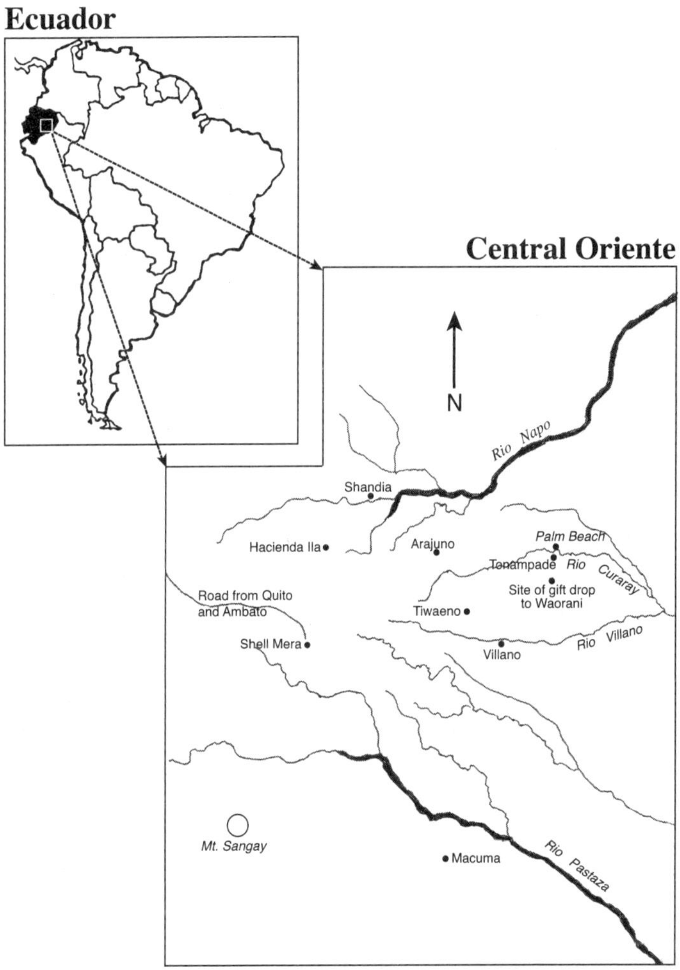
Ecuador
Central Oriente
N
Rio Napo
Shandia
Hacienda Ila
Arajuno
Palm Beach
Tonampade
Rio Curaray
Site of gift drop
to Waorani
Tiwaeno
Road from Quito
and Ambato
Shell Mera
Villano
Rio Villano
Mt. Sangay
Macuma
Rio Pastaza

Contents

Chapter 1

A Dangerous Task

"Tidonca's son is dead," Rachel Saint overheard one of the Waorani women say.

Rachel had been expecting the bad news, as the child had been sick for several days. Rachel rose wearily from her desk and went to find Tidonca.

Toucans squawked in the branches of the ironwood trees above and monkeys squealed in the distance as Rachel made her way along the trail that led to Tidonca's hut several hundred yards away from the main village clearing. By now the morning sun had burned away most of the cooling mist that had crept up overnight from the river. What mist remained diffused the scant rays of light that made it to the jungle floor.

Soon Rachel reached a small clearing beside the trail and found Tidonca sitting on a log outside the small thatched hut he called home. He was sharpening a spear made from a chonta palm, honing the barbs to sharp points. Rachel was surprised; she had expected Tidonca to be preparing a burial site for his dead son. "What are you doing, Tidonca?" she asked.

Tidonca looked up from sharpening his spear and replied flatly, "My son has died. Why should my worthless daughter live?"

A shiver ran down Rachel's spine. She knew that Tidonca was serious. Aucas often killed their daughters when a son died or buried children alive with their dead fathers. Rachel stepped back; her mind began to whirl. She had to do something. She could not stand by and let an innocent child be speared to death. But what could she do? She was a middle-aged American woman in the dense Amazon jungle, surrounded by a tribe of people with a reputation for being ruthless killers. But before she even realized it, Rachel was moving. She ran toward Tidonca, snatched the spear from his hands, and sprinted off into the jungle. It was a desperate move, and Rachel waited for the sting of a poisonous dart in her back from Tidonca's blowpipe, but it did not come. Instead Tidonca called after Rachel, "Nimu, leave me my spear."

"No, you are not going to kill your daughter with it," Rachel called back over her shoulder as she kept running.

Rachel wandered along tangled jungle tracks for several hours before finally deciding to return to her thatched hut with the spear. When she got there, she found Kimo, one of the other men of the tribe, standing outside. She expected him to be angry with her or, worse, use his own spear against her. Instead, when Kimo saw Rachel, a smile animated his weathered, coffee-brown face.

"Tidonca is very angry with you," Kimo reported. "But I have told him you are my friend. To spear you, he will have to spear me first."

Rachel hardly knew what to say. For the first time ever, she was witnessing one member of the tribe standing up to another over the way things had been done for generations. She could only hope that Kimo's brave stand did not get him killed.

Thankfully Tidonca went ahead with the burial, and no blood was shed.

The following morning Rachel picked up Tidonca's spear and made her way along the trail to his hut. She found him once again sitting on the log outside. Rachel walked gingerly toward him, the spear in her outstretched hands. Would he use that spear to kill her? After all, Rachel had humiliated him when she snatched it away in the first place. He was a Waorani warrior, and she, a foreign woman, had taken his spear. Tidonca nodded grudgingly, took the spear, and walked into his hut. Rachel stood there for a moment. The crisis had passed.

Rachel breathed a sigh of relief after the incident. Innocent life had been saved, and she hoped that her actions would serve as an object lesson to the Waorani that a human life was a sacred thing to be protected, not mindlessly and brutally destroyed.

Rachel herself knew from firsthand experience the devastating effects of the Waorani's brutal killing sprees. Now, with God's help, she was determined to stop the killing and show the members of the tribe that there was a better way to live. It was a treacherous task that she had embarked upon, a task that she could never have anticipated as a small girl growing up on the outskirts of Philadelphia.

Chapter 2

A New Home for the Family

In November 1918, Rachel Saint sat quietly on a box in the curved driveway of her grandparents' mansion. This was more than could be said for her four brothers. Her two older brothers, Sam and Phil, were playing hide-and-seek among the various trunks and bags stacked in the driveway, while younger brothers Dan and David cried because they were too small to join in the game.

Rachel felt like crying herself. At four years of age she was aware that she was leaving behind everything that was familiar to her. Born in Wyncote, Pennsylvania, she had spent her life thus far living with her parents and their growing brood in a small cottage on her grandparents' estate. She loved her grandparents' mansion, with its deep Persian rugs and pale, velvet furnishings. Most of the time Rachel was the only grandchild allowed in the house. Her grandmother had banned the boys from the place after they had used the davenport as a springboard to fly into the air and out through an open window onto a pile of feather cushions they had placed on the front veranda.

Rachel's grandfather Josiah Proctor had been an inventor who in the late nineteenth century had invented machinery that made woolen mills operate more efficiently. Josiah had founded a company called Proctor and Schwartz (which later became known as Proctor Silex) to make and market the machinery. But Josiah had recently died, and after the funeral Rachel had overheard her parents discussing the fact that the family of four boys and one girl was getting too large for the small cottage. If the family moved out into the country, her parents reasoned, everyone would have room to grow and stretch. And that is how Rachel came to be sitting among the trunks and bags in the driveway of the Proctor estate. This was the day the Saint family was moving to Huntingdon Valley, a small country town outside of Abington. Rachel hardly knew what to expect, but her mother had tried to make the move into an adventure. So when Rachel was not thinking about how much she was going to miss her grandmother, she had to admit that living in the countryside sounded interesting.

As it turned out, Rachel loved her new home in the country from the moment the family arrived there. The new house was three stories high, with a ledge along the roof on which the children were allowed to sleep during the summer months. A fifty-foot length of rope, on which Rachel loved to swing, hung from a tree in the backyard. As well, Rachel's father, Lawrence Saint, built a roller coaster that led down from the third story of the house and was the swiftest way to get from upstairs to the kitchen.

Surrounding the house in every direction were places where the children could play and make up all kinds of games. The Pennypack Creek flowed nearby and was a perfect spot for swimming in the summer and ice skating during the snowy winter months. Although Rachel liked to ice skate, her favorite winter activity was leading a tobogganing expedition each year on her birthday, January 2.

Another activity that Rachel liked was riding in the old electric car the Saint family had inherited from Grandfather Proctor. The great, lumbering vehicle was powered by enormous lead acid batteries mounted in the front and the rear and was controlled from the backseat, where it was steered by a tiller rather than a steering wheel. From time to time Rachel's father would back it out of the barn and the family would all clamber in for a ride through the countryside. Most of all Rachel liked the times when just she and her parents got to ride in the car and the boys stayed behind at the house to play.

With so many children to care for and no maids to help her, Rachel's mother, Katherine, developed a unique system of feeding and clothing everyone.

She cooked an enormous quantity of one food and kept feeding it to everyone until someone complained. Then she would make a change and prepare another dish. Rachel, being the only girl, had her own clothes, but the boys all shared what they had. Katherine Saint would wash and dry the boys' clothes and then hang them in a large downstairs room. From there the boys helped themselves to whatever fit them, and Rachel soon noticed that the brother who got up first seemed to be the best dressed for the day.

Rachel's childhood in Huntingdon Valley passed in a whirl of activity and possibilities. The family's Christian beliefs were at the center of everything the family did. They attended church at least twice on Sunday, and then there were the Wednesday-night prayer meetings, which they often walked miles to attend. The family also had daily Bible readings and prayer times, which all of the children joined in. The prayers were often about the family's need for food and other material things. There never seemed to be quite enough money to pay for all the necessities, since Lawrence Saint was a struggling stained-glass artist. But despite the lack of money, Rachel's mother did the best she could with what she had. She patched and repatched clothes and could stretch a pound of beans to feed the entire family. Sometimes there was nothing to eat in the house but milk and peanuts for a week or more at a time.

By the time Rachel was twelve, her mother had given birth to three more boys—Steve, Nate, and

Ben. Rachel and Nate shared a special bond, despite the fact that Nate was nine years younger than Rachel. Katherine and Lawrence Saint had brought up all of their children to be God-fearing, but Nate seemed to especially delight in the Bible stories and missionary tales that Rachel read to him, and he was always begging her for just one more story.

Reading these stories to her younger brother and sometimes acting them out was one of Rachel's favorite activities, as were the Sunday-afternoon family get-togethers. When the weather was good, Rachel's father insisted on leading everyone on hikes through the surrounding wheat fields and among groves of tall cedar trees. On rainy or snowy Sunday afternoons, the family settled in the parlor to sketch portraits and paint various landscapes. Drawing was a perfectly normal part of the Saint family's activities, and Rachel especially loved to hear her parents tell stories of their artistic heritage.

Rachel's grandfather James Saint had been a gifted portrait artist back in the 1860s in Pittsburgh. But since there had not been much demand for oil paintings back then, he had eked out a living traveling around to fairs and expositions, cutting out silhouettes of faces and selling them for a penny each. As a result of this itinerant lifestyle, Rachel's father had grown up in poor surroundings and had left home at fifteen to make a living selling newspapers, with the hope of one day becoming a successful artist. Lawrence Saint had moved to Philadelphia, where he volunteered his spare time teaching at a gospel mission in South Philadelphia. It was while volunteering there that he had met Rachel's mother, Katherine Proctor. Katherine had recently become a Christian, and as a result she, too, was volunteering her time at the mission school. It was the classic tale of a struggling, penniless young artist and a rich, beautiful young woman falling in love with each other, and Rachel never tired of hearing the story.

After some time Lawrence won an art scholarship to study in Europe, and Katherine suggested that she go along with him—as his wife. A hasty wedding was organized, and the couple spent their honeymoon in Paris. It was while he was in Paris, Rachel knew, that her father discovered his destiny in art—recreating the medieval stained-glass windows of Europe using the ancient techniques. The trouble was that no one was sure exactly what these ancient techniques were. So while Lawrence sketched countless stained-glass windows, Katherine translated numerous French texts in the hope that they might provide some clue as to how craftsmen using just a few simple tools had created such stunning windows.

Soon after moving back to the United States and into the house in Huntingdon Valley, Lawrence set up an art studio and began experimenting with various techniques for making stained glass. His quest was driven in part by the fact that the color and texture of the glass he could buy commercially was not of good enough quality for the windows he wanted to make. He experimented with combining various ingredients in a furnace he built in the backyard, with the goal of making the highest quality glass possible. Many times Rachel watched the disappointment in her father's eyes when a particularly promising recipe rendered inferior glass, dashing his hopes. But Lawrence was not a man to give up easily. His experimentation eventually paid off, and he began to produce high-quality glass. The glass was so superior that a crew from the Metropolitan Museum of Art in New York City came to the studio in Huntingdon Valley to film Lawrence Saint at work.

Although it was exciting to have a film crew film her father at work, fourteen-year-old Rachel really knew that all the experimentation had paid off when her father returned one day from a trip into Philadelphia. Lawrence had gone looking for work, and when he stepped through the door of the family home on his return, Rachel could see the excitement in his blue eyes.

"Come here, everyone. I have the most wonderful news to tell you," Lawrence said, hanging up his hat.

Katherine and the children gathered around, and then Lawrence went on. "I was sitting quietly on the train, riding into Philadelphia, when a stranger came up to me. He sat beside me, and he said, 'Your resemblance to the portraits of Christ is striking. I have to ask you, what is your name and what do you do?' So I told him, 'My name is Saint, and I make stained-glass windows for churches.' 'Well,' the man replied as he reached out to shake my hand, 'my name is Raymond Pitcairn, and I am building a cathedral. When can you start on my windows?'"

Rachel's mother clapped her hands. "Oh, Lawrence, that's wonderful! See, children. God has answered our prayers. Your father has work to do."

"And lots of it," Lawrence added. "The cathedral is the Bryn Athyn Cathedral in Philadelphia, and after that he says he wants me to work on the new National Cathedral being built at Mount Saint Alban in Washington, D.C."

Sam and Phil let out simultaneous whoops of joy, and Rachel heard Sam say under his breath, "Thank You, God. Now I will be able to learn to fly."

Rachel felt a glow of satisfaction as she thought of all the wonderful opportunities that a steady paycheck would afford the family. And, indeed, everyone benefited from the work her father did on the two beautiful new cathedrals. For once there was enough food in the house for everyone, and Sam got his flying lessons. But best of all, the children took turns traveling first into Philadelphia and then to Washington, D.C., with their father to admire his work.

It was on one of these trips to Washington, D.C., that Rachel was introduced to Mr. and Mrs. Parmalee, the elderly couple who were sponsoring the work on the stained-glass windows at the National Cathedral. Mrs. Parmalee, a millionaire in her own right, and Rachel liked each other instantly. Soon Rachel was spending a lot of time in the Parmalees' home. Since the couple had no children of their own, Mrs. Parmalee treated Rachel like a daughter. In fact, in 1931 Mrs. Parmalee suggested that she take Rachel on a trip to Great Britain for her upcoming eighteenth birthday. It was to be a "coming-out" trip, which many wealthy and eligible young women took in those days.

Rachel was delighted with the idea. She had never dreamed of being able to cross the Atlantic Ocean to see the British Isles. Plans for the trip were soon under way. Rachel's Grandmother Proctor sent bolts of fabric to be made into suitable dresses for a debutante. All of the fuss being made over her was new to Rachel, who had to admit that she enjoyed the beautiful dresses made from the fabric as well as the thought of traveling first class, staying in grand hotels, and eating sumptuous meals. However, Rachel had no idea that during her time away in Great Britain she would be faced with a decision that would direct the course of her entire life.

Chapter 3

"Her People"

The trip to Great Britain was just as Rachel imagined it would be, filled with interesting people and places to see. In true Saint style she took along a sketchpad wherever she went to record what she saw. While visiting Edinburgh, Scotland, she was particularly impressed with the statue "Fatigue" in Princes Street. Rachel was even more impressed when she learned that the sculptor was forty years of age before he had undertaken his first creative work. For some reason the thought that no matter how old a person was, he or she could learn new things inspired Rachel.

In London Mrs. Parmalee and Rachel toured many churches, where they saw the great stained-glass windows from the Middle Ages. As she viewed the windows, Rachel was reminded of her parents' telling of how overwhelmed and awed they had been on seeing Europe's stained-glass windows for the first time.

Throughout the trip Rachel and Mrs. Parmalee stayed in the finest hotels and shopped at the most exclusive stores. At first this was exciting to Rachel, but after a while the charm began to wear off. Rachel wondered about all the money that was being spent unnecessarily. Just one pot of tea and some scones at Harrods cost enough money to feed the entire Saint family for three days! By the end of the tour, Rachel was ready to return home.

Finally the two women boarded the Cunard Line's ship *Aquitania*—in a first-class cabin, of course—for the journey back to the United States. At lunch one day as the ship steamed across the Atlantic Ocean, Mrs. Parmalee's face grew serious. "Rachel, dear, have you enjoyed yourself?" Mrs. Parmalee asked.

"Why, yes," Rachel replied. "I have seen so many things I never dreamed I would see."

"Wonderful," Mrs. Parmalee said, reaching over to pat her hand. "You may have been raised in humble circumstances, but you have the fine instincts and family background that would make me proud to call you my daughter."

Rachel felt herself blushing. In her household of seven brothers, compliments were few and far between.

"In fact, that's what I wanted to talk to you about. I am getting older," Mrs. Parmalee sighed before going on, "and it's time to think of the future. We seem to be very compatible, you and I, so I have a proposition to make. If you will be my companion and help me with light duties, I will make you my heiress."

Rachel stared down at her teacup, unable to imagine what the correct response to such an offer might be. She had heard her father say that Mrs. Parmalee was worth over a million dollars, and now Mrs. Parmalee wanted to give all her money to Rachel!

Rachel did not speak for a while, and again Mrs. Parmalee reached over and patted her hand. "Well, dear, I know it's a lot to take in. Perhaps you will have an answer for me by the end of the voyage," she said.

Throughout the rest of the day, Rachel found herself scrutinizing her fellow first-class passengers. She listened in on their conversations during card games and watched as they danced at dinner. Was this really the life she had been born to live? Her grandmother Proctor would certainly say yes, as would Mrs. Parmalee. But Rachel knew that she had to make the decision for herself. She thought of her mother patching the boys' clothes by lamplight and telling them yet again that there was no meat for dinner or that they would have to eat biscuits and lard for breakfast and lunch. She thought of the way the coffee grounds were used three times before being discarded and how the whole family had to pool their money to buy pencils and paper at the start of each school year.

Life in the Saint family had been hard in some respects, Rachel could see that, but she knew that her mother had chosen that life. Her mother had done so mainly because she felt that God was calling her to it and because she loved Rachel's father so much. Even though her mother was a Wellesley College graduate and a student of fine arts, Rachel knew that in her heart her mother did not regret the life she had chosen. This knowledge brought Rachel face-to-face with the choice she had to make. Would she take the million-dollar inheritance and the opportunity to travel in style, or would she choose the unknown? Would she head out into the world with the love of her family but very little in the way of financial support?

That night Rachel got hardly any sleep. She heard the bells of the night watch and the rumble of the ship's horn sounding as the vessel passed through a fog bank. As daybreak approached, Rachel decided to creep out of her cabin and up on deck to see the sunrise. With any luck, the coastline of the United States might even be in view by now.

On deck a cool wind was blowing, and it sent a shiver down Rachel's spine. Rachel wrapped a woolen shawl closely around her. She was the only passenger out on the first-class deck. As the sun began to creep above the sea, barely above the horizon, its long, yellow rays reflected off the coastline of North America in the distance. The sight of the coast suddenly warmed Rachel, despite the wind.

With the first glimpse of the coastline, Rachel knew that she would have to make a decision. Well, not make it, exactly. Sometime in the night she had admitted to herself that the life of luxury was not for her. Deep in her heart she knew that God had a plan for her life and that it did not include sipping endless cups of tea and chatting idly. No, somehow Rachel knew that God was asking her to trust that He would lead her into some great adventure, not an adventure that would make her rich but a great adventure nonetheless.

As she rehearsed in her head the right way to tell Mrs. Parmalee of her decision so as not to offend her too much, Rachel was aware of something strange happening to her. It was as if she were not standing on the deck of the ship anymore but was instead standing in a jungle clearing, looking at a group of brown-skinned, half-naked people. The people beckoned for her to come to them.

As quickly as the scene came, it left. Rachel felt the hair on the back of her neck stand on end. She had read about many figures in the Bible, such as Abraham, King David, Isaiah, Paul, and John, who had experienced visions. Was that what she had just experienced? Without thinking about it, Rachel fell to her knees and closed her eyes. "God," she prayed, "I will give my whole life to You and go and be a missionary to those brown-skinned people if You want me to."

All morning as the *Aquitania* sailed closer to shore and then finally entered New York Harbor to dock, Rachel was preoccupied with thoughts of her vision. Who were those people, and when would she get to meet them?

Surprisingly Rachel found it effortless to tell Mrs. Parmalee that she did not want to be her heir. The two women parted company in Philadelphia as friends, even though Mrs. Parmalee had to admit that she could not understand how a girl could turn down such an opportunity.

Upon her return home to Huntingdon Valley, Rachel had a renewed sense of purpose. Although she continued to help her mother raise the younger boys, she also enrolled in Percy Crawford's evening Bible school. She loved studying at the school so much that, when she was twenty, she decided to enroll at the Philadelphia College of Bible.

As she studied, Rachel was convinced that somewhere in the world was a group of brown-skinned people in a jungle waiting for her to come to them. Soon after she graduated from Philadelphia College of Bible in 1936 at age twenty-two, Rachel applied to be a missionary. However, she was turned down because of a weak back. Rachel thought it ironic, since her back problems had never stopped her from being an active family helper or from studying her Bible. At first she was angry about the decision, but then she began to wonder whether "her people," as she called them, were not yet ready for her.

With this thought in mind, Rachel went to work at the Keswick Colony of Mercy, a halfway house for alcoholics located in rural New Jersey. Nothing could have been further from the life of ease Mrs. Parmalee had offered and which Rachel had turned down, but Rachel loved her work at the halfway house. She often laughed and told friends that being raised with seven brothers was the best training she could have had for the job. Sometimes in the course of her work she had to confront violent, drunken men and at other times talk such men out of committing suicide.

After 1941, with America firmly involved in the fighting of World War II, the problem of alcohol abuse seemed to Rachel to reach epidemic proportions. As a result of their involvement in the war, many men whose dreams were shattered turned to alcohol for comfort. But when their drinking got out of control, they would come to the mission seeking help. And Rachel was always willing and eager to help.

When she returned home for Christmas 1942, Rachel learned that her brother Nate, now nineteen years old, had enlisted in the army and was about to head off to Camp Luna in Las Vegas, New Mexico. Nate had been based at La Guardia Field in New York City, working as an aircraft mechanic for American Airlines, for whom their older brother Sam was now a pilot. During his spare time, Nate had taken flying lessons, and he hoped to transfer to the Army Air Corps after basic training and become a pilot. Rachel kept up to date on Nate's progress by letter and was pleased for her brother when he was indeed accepted into the Army Air Corps, where he was undergoing pilot training. Then disaster struck. When he was fourteen, Nate had suffered from osteomyelitis, and during pilot training, this old illness flared up again, forcing him to withdraw from the program and precluding him from being posted overseas. Still, Rachel was proud of the way her younger brother handled the disappointment. Nate kept his spirits up and trusted God and continued to serve his country as best he could. Instead of becoming a pilot, Nate was assigned to be an aircraft mechanic, working on C-47 cargo planes and other aircraft at various army bases around the United States.

In the meantime Rachel's older brother Phil, an evangelist who traveled and spoke around the United States, had decided to become a missionary to Argentina. Rachel could not help but feel a little envious when she heard the news. She kept in touch with Phil by letter and was particularly interested in hearing of his exploits in South America. She wondered whether "her people" were somewhere on that continent.

The years of working at the Keswick Colony of Mercy rolled by, first five, then ten, then twelve. Rachel was thirty-four years old, and most of her friends predicted that she would work for the halfway house until she retired. But something was stirring within her. Rachel had just read a series of articles on a visionary man named Cameron Townsend and his new program, the Summer Institute of Linguistics, held at the University of Oklahoma in Norman. Rachel had known about Townsend's work for some time, but as she read the articles about him, she was impressed with the way his ministry was starting to take off. Townsend actually had three separate ministries under him—the Summer Institute of Linguistics (SIL), Wycliffe Bible Translators, and the fledgling Jungle Aviation and Radio Services (JAARS). All three organizations had separate roles to fulfill but worked together to bring the gospel to groups of people who had never heard it before.

At the same time, in 1948 Rachel received a letter from Nate saying that he was now serving with a missionary organization called Missionary Aviation Fellowship (MAF). The letter stated that Nate and his new wife, Marj, would soon be moving to Ecuador to start an operations base for the organization across the Andes Mountains in the Amazon jungle in the east of the country. From there they planned to use airplanes to serve the various isolated mission stations dotted across the region.

Suddenly, with one brother already serving as a missionary in South America and another brother about to head there, once again the whole question of missionary service loomed before Rachel. And after reading the articles about Cameron Townsend, Rachel found the idea of studying to decipher and learn unknown languages greatly appealing. Ever since seeing the vision of the brown-skinned people in the jungle sixteen years before on the ship returning from Great Britain, Rachel had been convinced that she would one day take the gospel to a group of people who had never heard it before. And that meant that the group probably did not speak a language that those in the outside world could recognize. Now Rachel was beginning to feel that the time was right to pursue becoming a missionary and fulfilling the vision. She was encouraged by a verse from Paul's letter to the Romans: "Those who have never been told of Him shall see, and those who have never heard shall understand" (Romans 15:21).

Rachel took the plunge and applied to attend the Summer Institute of Linguistics. She was delighted when word came that she had been accepted for the course.

Those who had thought Rachel would stay working at the Keswick Colony of Mercy until she retired were surprised when they received an invitation to her farewell. Many people—family, friends, coworkers, and those she had helped over the years—came to wish Rachel well in her new venture. Rachel was touched by the tributes of the people who attended the farewell. And while she was sad to be leaving behind both people and a place she had grown to love and appreciate, she was excited about what lay ahead.

The 1948 Summer Institute of Linguistics was every bit as interesting and challenging as described in the articles Rachel had read about the school. Rachel was impressed with the teachers, particularly Ken Pike, and the breadth of their linguistic knowledge. Ken had attended the second Summer Institute of Linguistics held in 1935. He had gone on to earn a doctorate in linguistics and now served as the president of Summer Institute of Linguistics (SIL).

Rachel enjoyed every single day of the eleven-week course as she came to grips with the basics of how to listen to and then learn a native language.

She had many practical things to learn. Classes were divided into three topics. The first topic was phonetics, which taught the students how to listen to the different sounds of a language and write them down. Sometimes this was difficult to do because some languages had gulping, humming, and clicking sounds that were not easy to write down using the English alphabet. Regardless, this was an important skill to master. The second topic was morphology, which taught the students how to find out what words were related to each other in a foreign language. While the English language used prefixes and suffixes to slightly change the meaning of a word, other languages did not, so it was important to know how to discover what words were linked to each other. The final topic was syntax, which taught the students how to discover the way a sentence was put together in the foreign language.

The learning was challenging, but as the school progressed, Rachel became convinced that she was moving toward her destiny. By the time the Summer Institute of Linguistics was finally over, she knew that the next step was to become a competent Bible translator. When Rachel had accomplished this feat, it would then be time for her to set out and find the brown-skinned people she had seen in her vision. Rachel was certain that they were somewhere in the jungles of South America waiting for her.

Chapter 4

Were These the People?

The next step on the road to Rachel's becoming a competent Bible translator and missionary involved attending the three-month-long Jungle Camp. As its name implied, Jungle Camp was located in the jungle near El Real in the state of Chiapas in southern Mexico. Rachel had first heard of the place in letters from her brother Nate. Two years before, in 1946, a small airplane that serviced Jungle Camp had crashed upon landing at the jungle airstrip, and Nate had been sent to El Real to rebuild the damaged aircraft. In his letters to Rachel, Nate had described the rustic nature of Jungle Camp. When Rachel finally arrived there, she discovered that her brother had not exaggerated his description of the place.

Jungle Camp consisted of a group of mud huts situated among the trees beside a river. The jungle, Rachel learned, spread all the way east to Mexico's border with Guatemala and beyond. Rachel shared one of the small mud huts with another woman, while a second mud hut nearby had a single stove in it and served as the camp kitchen.

The daily schedule was demanding. Every morning Rachel was up at six. Breakfast was served at seven, followed by linguistics study from eight till ten. Then it was time for two hours of work in the garden, hoeing the damp jungle floor in an attempt to grow vegetables to eat. Lunch was served at twelve thirty, followed by another hour of linguistics study. The rest of the afternoon was then taken up with other tasks as well as more linguistics study.

Jungle Camp was unlike anything Rachel had ever experienced. It was one long test of survival. And that was the point. The camp was designed to be a sort of boot camp where prospective missionaries were taught how to survive and live and work in rugged, remote, and primitive locations. So, as well as studying linguistics and doing chores, Rachel found herself paddling a heavily laden canoe through white-water rapids, hiking over rough mountain passes, hunting for food amid the jungle foliage, constructing a makeshift hut without tools, and learning how to treat snakebites and use penicillin, the newest drug on the market. She and the other students also completed a nine-day hike through the jungle to observe the work of Phil and

Mary Baer. The Baers were Wycliffe missionaries serving among the Lacandón Indians situated near the Guatemalan border. Rachel was impressed with the work the Baers were doing with the Lacandóns and hoped that when her turn came she, too, would be an effective and fruitful missionary. The nine-day hike was followed by a four-day solo experience in the jungle, where Rachel got to put all the survival skills she had learned to work.

Each day at Jungle Camp seemed to bring some new adjustment or challenge for Rachel. Most had to do with the local animals. Rats scurried around the wooden beams in the kitchen, and wild burros (donkeys) sneaked into the compound at night and ate any laundry accidentally left on the clothesline. To make matters worse, poisonous snakes seemed to lie in ambush at every turn, and the mosquitoes were ubiquitous, swarming around and biting Rachel everywhere she went.

Despite the hardships, Rachel was not deterred. As hard as the experience of Jungle Camp might be, she knew it was preparing her for what she believed was her destiny for the rest of life. She was also grateful for her childhood. All the hiking, swimming, and boisterous games she had played with her brothers had helped to prepare her for the rigors of jungle life.

As Jungle Camp progressed, Rachel gleaned all the information she could from visiting SIL and Wycliffe workers. She learned that the organization's main focus at present had moved from the Indians of Mexico to the Indians of Peru and that Wycliffe missionaries were also now working in New Guinea and moving out from there into the remote islands of the Pacific.

When Jungle Camp finally ended, Rachel received her assignment: she was being sent to Peru to work among the Piro Indians in the northeastern part of the country. There she would relieve Esther Matteson, an SIL missionary who was about to return home on furlough. Rachel was excited about her new assignment, especially since she would have the opportunity to stop off in Ecuador on the way and visit Nate and his wife, Marj, who were both now serving there with Missionary Aviation Fellowship.

From a small, remote airstrip in the jungle at Shell Mera, Nate was using an airplane to fly out and service the various mission stations dotted throughout the Oriente, as the jungle region of Ecuador east of the Andes Mountains was called. The Oriente formed the western reaches of the Amazon Basin. For two thousand miles the jungle ran eastward from Ecuador all the way across South America to the Atlantic coast of Brazil.

In truth, Rachel's brother wasn't flying anywhere at present because of an unfortunate accident. A severe downdraft had caught his Stinson aircraft as he took off from Quito, Ecuador's capital, causing the plane to crash. Nate had survived the ordeal but had to wear a cast that encompassed his upper body while a compression fracture of one of the vertebrae in his back healed. Nate had written to Rachel and told her all about the accident, noting that the recovery from his injury would be long and slow. As a result Rachel was eager to go to Ecuador and encourage her little brother. She was also eager to see her new niece, to whom Marj had recently given birth.

Rachel flew to Quito, situated on the equator high in the Andes Mountains. From there she caught a bus for the long trip down the eastern side of the Andes to the small community of Shell Mera. As the bus bumped and twisted its way south past Mount Cotopaxi toward Ambato, Rachel chatted in Spanish to the passengers sitting around her.

Every half hour or so the bus would grind to a halt in a cloud of dust, amidst a chorus of excited shouts. Local people clambered either on or off the bus, and the loudness of their shouting depended on how much luggage they stowed on the vehicle's roof. As each passenger climbed aboard, he or she heaved up onto the bus roof bags, crates, and sacks containing everything from vegetables to bantam hens. It was a lot more difficult, though, to get these things down than it was to toss them up. Sometimes an item of luggage would get stuck at the bottom of the pile and everything had to be unloaded to retrieve it. It seemed to Rachel to take forever to do this, and she, along with everyone else on the bus, craned her neck to see out the window to make sure that all of her belongings were loaded back onto the top of the bus and not left behind.

At every stop the bus made, vendors took advantage of the captive, hungry passengers. Of course, with her milky-white complexion, Rachel stood out from the other passengers. As a result the vendors seemed to steer themselves straight to her, offering to sell her all sorts of tasty goodies, everything from homemade lemonade poured into old beer bottles to whole, roasted guinea pigs, complete with hair, paws, and teeth. Rachel just waved them off.

At lunchtime the bus arrived in Ambato, the so-called gateway to the Oriente. From Ambato the route veered to the east and dropped steeply through the town of Baños and on into the eastern jungle. As the bus descended from the mountains, Rachel watched the scenery outside change. The barren, rocky mountain vistas had now been replaced by lush, green vegetation laced through with masses of orchids that grew right up to the edge of the rutted road.

As they bumped along, the snowcapped peak of the volcano Mount Sangay came into view. Nate had described the mountain to Rachel in one of his letters, and now, with it clearly in sight, Rachel knew that she was getting close to her destination.

Finally the bus navigated one more dogleg bend in the road and rolled along for a half mile before screeching to a halt outside a general store that bore a sign reading "Shell Mera." Rachel was relieved and delighted that after twelve hours on the bus the arduous journey was finally at an end. She was even more delighted when waiting outside in front of the store was her brother Nate.

"Welcome to Shell Mera," Nate greeted Rachel, who embraced her brother as best she could, since his whole upper body was still sheathed in a cast. While they waited for Rachel's bag to be off-loaded from the roof of the bus, Nate explained that the small settlement, which consisted of about thirty buildings in all, had been hacked out from the jungle by the Shell Oil Company, hence its name. The place served as the company's main base for oil exploration in the Oriente.

Once her bag had been unloaded, Rachel set out with Nate for Shell Merita, the name Nate and Marj had given to their house at the end of the airstrip. Nate led the way, loping along as best he could in his cast. Rachel followed him along the road the bus had just driven down. The road ran parallel to a long, neatly cleared airstrip. At the end of the airstrip on the other side of the road was a tin-roofed house. "That's home, sweet home," Nate pointed out.

Soon Rachel was sitting in the lounge of Shell Merita, bouncing her new niece Kathy in her arms and looking out on the wonderful view of Mount Sangay that the room afforded. Although Rachel had not seen Nate for several years, as they laughed and talked together, the years seemed to fall away, and Rachel soon felt the same connection she had always had with her younger brother.

Nate and Marj listened attentively as Rachel told them all about her experiences at the Summer Institute of Linguistics in Oklahoma and at Jungle Camp in Mexico. Rachel also told them about her being assigned to Peru and how excited she was about getting there and beginning her career as a missionary. Then Nate explained to her all about life in the Oriente and how, once his back was healed, he hoped to get a new aircraft and begin flying again to the outlying mission stations. He explained about the various tribes that lived in the Oriente and about the different mission organizations and missionaries who worked among them, some of whom had become his close friends.

"But there's one tribe no one is working among," Nate said.

"Who are they, and why has no missionary taken up the challenge of reaching them with the gospel?" Rachel inquired.

"They're a tribe called the Aucas," Nate said, "and they have a reputation for killing all strangers who enter their territory. No one has ever been able to live with them."

Despite the Aucas' fearsome reputation, Rachel felt goose bumps forming on her arms as her brother spoke. Was this the group she had seen in her vision all those years ago? Were these the people waiting for her to bring them the gospel?

That night as Rachel lay in the tiny guest bedroom of Shell Merita, she thought about the Auca Indians who lived perhaps only a few miles from where she was staying. As she thought about the tribe, she began to feel that these were indeed the people she had seen in her vision. Yet she could not imagine how she was going to reach them. For one thing, Wycliffe Bible Translators and SIL had no mission base in Ecuador, and since the Aucas killed outsiders on contact, she had no idea how to convince them that she wanted to be their friend.

Before drifting off to sleep, Rachel prayed that God would somehow bring together the circumstances that would make her dream of reaching them with the gospel a reality.

In the meantime Rachel had plenty to occupy her time. After spending a week with Nate and Marj and baby Kathy, she continued on her way to Peru, where she settled in among the Piro Indians. Soon after her arrival there, Esther Matteson left for the United States on furlough. After Esther's return from furlough, Rachel decided it was time for a new challenge. She had hoped to go and live among the Murato Indians, a group who had never heard the gospel, and learn their language and translate the Scriptures into it. However, since no other missionary was available to go with Rachel and support her in this new venture, she had to abandon her plan. Although Rachel was deeply disappointed by this outcome, her disappointment soon turned to joy when she learned of an opportunity among the Shapra Indians.

The Shapras were a subgroup of the Candoshi Indian tribe, as were the Muratos, and they spoke a similar dialect of the Candoshi language. The Shapras were headhunters whose territory was located deep in the jungle along the Pushaga River, close to Peru's border with Ecuador.

In 1950 Doris Cox and Loretta Anderson had settled among the Shapras and begun learning their language. Now they were translating the New Testament into that language. However, since both Doris and Loretta were due to return home on furlough,

Rachel volunteered to go and work among the Shapra Indians while first Loretta and then Doris returned home.

As Rachel soon learned, even getting to Shapra territory was no easy feat. The first leg of the journey involved a five-hour trip in a small floatplane that flew over the dense jungle of eastern Peru. Rachel was relieved when the pilot finally circled the plane and brought it down for a landing on the Morona River. She was glad to get out and stretch her legs. But she soon discovered that she was trading one confined space for another for the rest of the journey. She took her place in the middle of a cramped dugout canoe, and soon they were off again. This time they paddled up the Pushaga River for eight hours before finally reaching Shapra territory. Rachel was delighted that the long journey was finally over, and she moved into the small, thatch-roofed house that Doris and Loretta had built. The floor of the house sat on stilts three feet above the ground, and the sides were mostly open.

Rachel enjoyed living and working among the Shapras. In a letter she wrote to friends about six weeks after arriving among the Shapra Indians, she noted,

> The Shapras are likeable Indian folk—handsome too, especially when they get their bright feathers out and comb their hair and primp and paint up. We find in them a character that we respect. We find it hard to

> believe that our Chief has avenged the killing of two of his brothers; that a pretty little young wife choked her first baby to death after her husband died. She wanted to marry again but no one would take her while she had the baby to care for.
>
> This jungle is a dream of nature's beauty—but a red sunset or rainbow here means certain death for someone, and the call of a certain bird is an ill omen. At night when the men have to be away, the women come with their children and sleep on the floor beside us. They are afraid of the evil spirits. Although we cannot tell them much yet, they know we are not afraid and they feel safe with us.

Rachel particularly liked getting to know Tariri, the chief of the tribe. The chief gave Rachel the Indian name Tiyotari. Rachel and Chief Tariri spent many hours together talking. Tariri boasted to Rachel about how many people he had killed in his lifetime and backed up his claim by showing Rachel the severed heads of his unfortunate victims. Tariri also explained about the Shapras' beliefs.

"The Candoshi trust in the boa for *arotama,* the power of a long life, Tiyotari," Tariri said one day. He then explained how a warrior, when he saw a boa in the jungle, would hit it with a stick and tie a vine around it. Then he would drag the serpent to a clearing and tie the vine to the ground and cover the snake with palm leaves so that it could not escape.

Then the warrior would lie down beside the boa and sleep and dream. In his dream the boa would come to him in the form of a man and give him something shiny to swallow—*arotama,* the power over life and his enemies. "Our ancestors said that the boa does not die; it just goes on living and living. That is why it has the power of *arotama,* and if you dream with a boa, you, too, will live like he does." The chief also explained to Rachel how the jaguar and the hawk could also give the power of *arotama.*

Rachel listened attentively to all Chief Tariri had to tell her. He told how tobacco smoke, along with chants and incantations, was used to overcome the power of the boa, especially when someone was ill or dying.

Over time, as Chief Tariri and Rachel continued to talk together, they became good friends. But one thing puzzled Rachel. Although the chief had allowed Doris and Loretta to live among his tribe, he had little respect for what they said. Why hadn't he killed them, Rachel wondered, or at least run them off from the village? One day Rachel asked the chief why this was.

"Ah, Tiyotari, if two men had come, I would have killed them both and taken their heads," Chief Tariri answered. "And if a man and a woman had come, I would have speared him and taken her as a wife. But two women came, calling me "brother." What could I do but protect them and let them live among us."

It was a chilling and honest answer that made Rachel glad she was a woman. Yet despite the chief's comments and the fact that headhunters surrounded her at every turn, Rachel felt strangely safe living among the Shapras. Her twelve years of working with vagrants and alcoholics had taught her to see past a person's behavior and value the person as a human being. As she did this, it was not long before Chief Tariri began asking questions about God and the outside world. Rachel answered his questions as honestly and simply as she could, always sharing some new point about the gospel in the process.

Following their chief's lead, other members of the tribe began to pay attention to what the missionary women among them were saying about a God who lived far away in a place that He wanted to take them to when they died.

Finally, after nearly a year away, Doris returned to her work among the Shapra Indians. With Doris's return, Rachel decided it was time to take a month's break before Loretta left for her furlough. Rather than travel all the way back to the United States, Rachel decided to return to Ecuador and stay with Nate and Marj for the month. Marj had recently given birth to a son, Steve, and Rachel was sure that she could do with some help around the mission station. Besides, Rachel wanted to find out whether anyone had learned more about the Auca Indians.

Chapter 5

"Those Are Your People Down There"

When Rachel arrived in Quito in late 1951, snow was clinging to the jagged Andean peaks that rose above the city. The slight chill in the air was refreshing after the steamy jungle heat of Peru. Nate was waiting to greet Rachel, and the two of them took some time to explore the city. As they wandered through the Mercado de Santa Clara, looking at the brightly painted balsa wood birds, cedar statues, bundles of dried herbs, and enormous bunches of freshly cut flowers, Rachel peppered her brother with questions about the Auca Indians. Had any missionary gone to live among them yet? Were they still hostile to strangers?

Nate told Rachel that the Aucas were as hostile as ever to outsiders and explained how they had recently attacked a number of Quichua Indians and Ecuadorians living on the borders of their territory. "In fact, there's a man living here in the city who I think you'll find interesting to talk to, Sis."

The following day Rachel followed Nate up the winding stone pathway that led to a white, stuccoed, two-story house. "He used to be stationed at Arajuno, so he's been in pretty close quarters with the Aucas," Nate said.

"Thanks for arranging this visit," Rachel told Nate as they stood in the tiled entranceway.

Nate knocked loudly on the large wooden door, which soon was swung open by a ten-year-old house girl. The girl smiled shyly and led Rachel and Nate into a wide, sparsely furnished room with polished wooden floors. A large fan whirled overhead, filling the room with a gentle breeze. Soon a stockily built man strolled into the room. He extended his hand to Nate.

"Dan Warburton," the man said with a distinctive Texas drawl. "You must be Nate Saint. I've heard a lot about you."

Nate shook Dan's hand and then introduced Rachel. Soon the three of them were sitting in overstuffed leather chairs, drinking iced tea.

Dan explained that he was an engineer with the Shell Oil Company and had been stationed at Arajuno when the company was exploring for oil there. He told them that Arajuno was located just outside Auca territory, but that had not stopped the Aucas from attacking the Shell workers. Over the years a number of European and Quichua Indian workers based at Arajuno had been speared to death.

"In the end, it just wasn't worth it," Dan explained. "We couldn't keep workers anymore. Oil's one thing, but the number of lives of Shell workers lost in the Oriente since the company started drilling there…it makes you think twice. In the end the company decided to pull out of the area altogether."

After gulping down some iced tea, Dan went on. "After one attack I found this headdress left behind by one of the Aucas." He walked over to the sideboard, opened a drawer, and pulled out the feathered object.

As Rachel took the headdress from Dan, her heart began to pound. She could scarcely believe it. The headdress was almost identical to the one Chief Tariri wore. Perhaps there were other similarities between the Auca and the Shapra Indians. Maybe their two languages were not that different. Could the Auca language be a dialect of Candoshi, as was the Shapra language?

The headdress filled Rachel with hope. Perhaps, she reasoned, God had sent her to the Shapras to prepare her to enter the Auca tribe. Until very recently the Shapra Indians had also been cold-blooded killers. But now their chief and many in the tribe were becoming open to the gospel, and the endless cycle of killing was beginning to die down. Would that happen to the Aucas soon as well?

"I told you meeting Dan Warburton would be interesting, didn't I?" Nate said as they left the house.

Rachel nodded. "It gave me such hope for the Aucas."

"So you really believe that the Lord has called you to work with the Aucas?" Nate asked.

"More than ever," Rachel replied.

Two days later Rachel and Nate were back in the jungle at Shell Mera, where Rachel got acquainted with her six-month-old nephew, Steve.

In the evening Rachel, Nate, and Marj would sit in the lounge of Shell Merita and talk. As Mount Sangay spewed steam and lava in the distance, Nate talked excitedly about his work. He explained that when the Shell Oil Company pulled out of the Oriente, the company sold the airstrip and the land around Shell Merita cheaply to Missionary Aviation Fellowship (MAF). The rest of the buildings had been bought by the Gospel Missionary Union, which had established the Berean Bible Institute in the buildings to train local Indian Christians.

Nate also told Rachel how his airplane had become an indispensable lifeline to the missionaries dotted throughout the Oriente. "I've even worked out a way to talk to those on the ground when there is no airstrip or I can't land for some reason," he said.

"And what's that?" Rachel asked.

"I call it my bucket drop. I bank the plane into a circle above the person I want to communicate with, and then I lower a telephone line. On the end of the line is a bucket with a telephone inside. Once I have played out all the cord, I put the plane into a tighter circle until the bucket hovers still at the end of the line. Then the person can pick up the phone, and we can talk. It works wonderfully," Nate said.

"It's an ingenious maneuver," Marj added. "He even received a letter of commendation and 250 dollars from the general manager of the Beech Aircraft Company for what they officially refer to as his 'spiral-line technique.'"

Rachel was most impressed.

"I have another invention to show you tomorrow," Nate added.

The following morning, after breakfast, Nate led Rachel out to the hangar that sat beside Shell Merita. Inside was MAF's four-seater Piper Pacer aircraft.

"The physics of flying are pretty simple, Sis," Nate said. "An airplane's propeller corkscrews through the air, pulling the plane along with it. As the plane is pulled forward, the movement of air over and under the wings creates lift, which keeps the plane aloft. But when the engine stops, the propeller stops, and the plane's forward motion quickly slows. When this happens, the lift under the wings is reduced, and the plane begins to lose altitude. If a pilot is flying over an open field or a road when this happens, he may be able to glide the plane in for an emergency landing. But when it happens over the jungle, nothing can be done to avoid hitting the trees.

"Airplane engines are usually well maintained, so when an engine does stop in flight, it's usually not a problem with the engine itself. Ninety-nine percent of the time when an engine stops, it's because the fuel is contaminated or has stopped flowing to the engine. The fuel might stop flowing for a number of reasons, but often the biggest cause is pilot error. A pilot changes plans in the middle of a flight to answer an emergency call or for some other reason, only to discover after he's committed to the change of plan that he doesn't have enough fuel to go the extra distance.

"It's a big issue out here in the Oriente, so I did some thinking about the problem. Eventually I came up with this device." Nate walked over and laid his hand on a device attached to the wing strut. "I call it my 'tin can lifesaver.'"

"How does it work?" Rachel inquired.

"It's pretty simple. It's a tank I fashioned from two of Marj's cooking-oil cans. It holds three gallons of gas, and this copper tube leads from the tank to the intake manifold on the engine. If for some reason I run out of fuel or the engine begins to starve for fuel, I can pull a rod on the control panel inside. The rod opens this valve, and the fuel from the three-gallon tank begins to flow to the engine, bringing it back to life. It works like a charm. It's not much fuel, but it's enough to get you to safety in most cases. I fashioned this cowling from a piece of balsa wood to make it more aerodynamic," Nate added, running his hand across the painted cowling.

Rachel thought about Grandpa Proctor, who would have been impressed. As an inventor himself, Grandpa Proctor would have been proud of his grandson Nate's ingenuity.

"I even have a patent for the device," Nate said. "And with the device fitted, I now even fly over Auca territory, 'cause I know I can make it to safety in friendlier territory. Maybe it's time you went and saw where this tribe you feel called to lives."

Rachel could barely contain her excitement. An hour later, after Nate had fueled the Piper Pacer and checked it out, they were winging their way over the jungle. Twenty minutes after taking off from the airstrip at Shell Mera, Nate banked the plane to the right. "That's Arajuno down there," he pointed out.

Rachel peered down at the cluster of abandoned buildings below. In the two years since the Shell Oil Company had abandoned the place, the jungle had been slowly reclaiming Arajuno. Tentacles of vines were swallowing up the decaying buildings.

After he had circled Arajuno, Nate leveled off the Pacer and headed east. "Sis, those are your people down there. This is Auca territory."

Rachel felt goose bumps form on her arms. This was Auca territory. This was where she felt sure God was leading her.

"The boundaries of Auca territory are basically the Napo River," Nate said, pointing out the left side of the plane, "the Villano River," this time pointing out the right side of the plane, "the Arajuno River behind us, and ahead of us to the Peruvian border."

Rachel studied the terrain below. The jungle was dense, so dense that one could not see through the trees to the ground. Occasionally there were small clearings in the jungle, and Rachel could see that gardens had been planted in several of them. However, by the time Nate banked the airplane around and began heading back to Shell Mera, Rachel had not caught sight of any Aucas. Still she was excited to have finally seen the Aucas' home with her own eyes.

After a month in Ecuador, Rachel said good-bye to Nate and Marj and the children and began the journey back to Peru. During her stay in the Ecuadorian Oriente, she had tried to learn as much as she could about the Aucas, but she had to admit it wasn't much. Because of their fearsome reputation, information about the Auca way of life remained mostly shrouded in secrecy.

Back in Peru Rachel went once again to live among the Shapra Indians. Chief Tariri's eyes lit up when she finally arrived back, and soon the chief and Rachel picked up their long conversations where they had left off.

Shortly after Rachel's return to the Shapras, Loretta Anderson left for her furlough. While Loretta was gone, Rachel threw herself into helping Doris translate portions of Scripture into the Shapras' dialect. The work was rewarding, and it was made all the more rewarding by the fact that Chief Tariri seemed to be inching toward accepting the gospel and becoming a Christian. Rachel encouraged the chief, although occasionally she was disappointed when he lapsed back into his old ways. On those occasions she would challenge him with his behavior. She would tell him that God and His Son, Jesus

Christ, were more powerful than the old ways, more powerful than the boa and all the animals and spirits of the jungle. Each time Rachel talked to the chief this way, he listened carefully and took her words to heart.

As Rachel worked among the Shapras, the Aucas were never far from her mind, and when Loretta finally returned from her furlough, Rachel decided it was time to actively pursue going to work among the Auca Indians in Ecuador. Of course she had no idea how this would all work out, since neither Wycliffe Bible Translators nor SIL worked in Ecuador.

Finally, as April 1953—Rachel's departure date from the Shapras—approached, Rachel told Chief Tariri she would be leaving.

"But Tiyotari, where are you going?" the chief asked.

"I'm going to teach another group of people. They are called the Aucas, and they live across the border in Ecuador," Rachel replied.

Chief Tariri looked at Rachel with sad eyes. "But we want you here," he said.

"I cannot stay. I must go to the Aucas and tell them about God, as I have told you and your people about Him. I would like to stay with you, but I must go," Rachel said.

Several days before Rachel's departure, Chief Tariri came to Rachel. He gave her a gift—a headdress made of brightly colored toucan feathers just like the one he wore. The wing feathers of the bird had been woven together in the front to form a crownlike ring, and at the back, a long tail of feathers hung down. With tears in her eyes, Rachel accepted the gift. She would miss Chief Tariri.

"When will we ever see you again?" the chief asked.

Rachel was too choked with emotion to answer.

At 6:00 AM on the day of her departure, Rachel climbed into the dugout canoe for the trip down the Pushaga River to meet the airplane that would ferry her to the Wycliffe Bible Translators' jungle base camp at Yarinacocha. Chief Tariri and his family accompanied her on the five-hour trip downriver. When they arrived at the Morona River, the Wycliffe airplane was waiting for her. After an emotional good-bye to Chief Tariri and his family, Rachel climbed aboard the small plane. Soon the aircraft was buzzing over the dense carpet of jungle on its way to Yarinacocha. Finally, at 6:00 PM, after a refueling stop for the airplane, Rachel arrived at her destination, exhausted from her day of traveling and emotional good-byes.

The following evening Rachel went to the dining room at Yarinacocha to eat dinner. Cameron Townsend and his young wife, Elaine, greeted her as she came in the door. Rachel talked with them for a minute or two and then sat down at a table with Catherine Peeke and Mary Sargent, who had been her closest missionary neighbors while she was living with the Shapras. Catherine and Mary had been working among the Záparo Indians, who lived along the Pastaza River close to the Ecuadorian border.

Rachel knew the river because it flowed through Shell Mera to the north in Ecuador. As the women sat eating, Catherine casually asked Rachel, "Where are you going next?"

Rachel hesitated for a moment before she finally said, "I'm not going back to the Shapras. My new tribe is across the border."

"In Ecuador?" Catherine asked.

Rachel nodded. "Yes, in Ecuador. I'm going to work among the Aucas."

Catherine and Mary looked puzzled, and Rachel knew why.

"But Wycliffe isn't working there," Catherine finally exclaimed.

Once again Rachel nodded her head. "I know," she said.

Still puzzled, Catherine and Mary ate on in silence.

Rachel herself was puzzled. She felt that God was leading her to the Aucas, but the very missionary organization she served with did not work in Ecuador. She had no idea how God would work the situation out. She just trusted that eventually He would.

As dinner was drawing to a close, Cameron Townsend stood up. He cleared his throat to get everyone's attention. The dining room quickly fell silent, and all eyes were on Uncle Cam, as everyone affectionately called him. Rachel watched as Uncle Cam held up a letter he had just received. "I would like to read to you this letter that arrived today. It is from the Ecuadorian ambassador to the United States inviting SIL to come and work in Ecuador."

Rachel gasped. Catherine and Mary looked at her, wide-eyed. Rachel's heart pounded. *This is my opportunity,* she told herself. *God has opened the way for me to work with the Aucas!*

Chapter 6

Hacienda Ila

Rachel could hardly contain her excitement as she stepped out of the guest house where she was staying into the bright afternoon sun that beat down on Quito, Ecuador. Beside her stood Catherine Peeke. As the two women waited for a taxi to arrive, Rachel did not feel like chatting. Her mind was elsewhere. She hardly knew which was the more thrilling event to look forward to today—meeting with a man reputed to know more about the Auca tribe than anyone else in the world or being officially introduced to the president of Ecuador.

In the days since making the move to Ecuador, Rachel had tried hard to find a way to reach the Aucas. She realized that it would be too dangerous to attempt to make contact directly with the tribe in the jungle. She hoped, though, that somewhere in Ecuador she would find an Auca Indian who had fled the tribe for some reason and who would be willing to teach her the Auca language. As a result she and Catherine had asked around Quito to see whether anyone knew of an Auca who had left the tribe. In the course of her doing this, a government official had recommended don Carlos Sevilla. "He knows more about the Aucas than anyone else," the official had said. "He has a hacienda in the jungle near their territory, and everyone calls him the Daniel Boone of Ecuador."

Soon a taxi arrived, and Rachel and Catherine climbed in. They gave the cab driver the address, and soon they were zooming through the narrow, bumpy streets. After a few minutes the driver brought the taxi to a halt outside a large, stuccoed house, much like the house in which Rachel had visited Dan Warburton three and a half years before. The house was don Carlos Sevilla's town home, where he stayed for several months each year.

Rachel and Catherine eagerly strode up to the front door and knocked. A house girl opened the door and let them inside. A few moments later don Carlos strolled into the room. He made an impressive sight. He was tall, muscular, and square-shouldered. His eyes were bright blue, and his once dark hair was streaked with gray. He politely introduced himself and guided Rachel and Catherine to a courtyard at the back of the house, where they all sat down in firm, straight-backed wooden chairs around a low table. Rachel and Catherine told don Carlos a little about their backgrounds. Rachel then went on to tell him how she hoped to one day live among the Aucas and share the gospel with them. She explained that she and Catherine had been directed to him because he supposedly knew more about the Aucas than anyone else in the country.

Don Carlos listened quietly while Rachel spoke. When she had finished, he laughed nervously.

"You cannot be serious," don Carlos exclaimed. "This would not be a wise course of action. No one lives among the Aucas. They are unpredictable and savage. You will surely be killed if you try. You are right when you say I know much about the Aucas. I have had much contact with them, but alas, this is all it has got me."

With that, don Carlos pulled up his loose cotton shirt. His torso was a maze of scars. "I have fought hand to hand with the Aucas," he continued, "and I am lucky to have survived to tell about it. Once I walked for eight days through the jungle to safety after being speared by an Auca warrior. So when I say these people are wild and unpredictable, I speak from experience."

Don Carlos paused for a moment and then continued. "I went in 1914 to live in the Oriente, where I established Hacienda Capricho in the jungle along the Rio Curaray. There I grew cotton and rice. But this location was inside Auca territory, and they would not let me or my workers alone. We were constantly stalked and attacked by them. Finally, in

1918, their savagery became too much. While I was away here in Quito, the Aucas attacked Hacienda Capricho and speared to death all of my workers. That was when I decided I could no longer stay there and grow crops. So I abandoned the hacienda and established a new one, Hacienda Ila, on the banks of the Anzu River, well away from Auca territory. There I employed many people, most of them Quichua Indians. I sent groups of my workers out into the jungle to collect rubber from the trees. I gave them instructions to be as kind as possible to any Aucas they encountered, to extend the hand of friendship."

Don Carlos shook his head. "But the Aucas do not understand friendship as you or I understand it. All they understand is killing. And over the years they have ambushed and killed many of my workers. And so you see, when I say this idea of yours—two American women living among the Aucas—is crazy and can only lead to certain death, I speak from long experience with this tribe. I urge you not to move ahead with this plan."

Rachel sat silently for a moment before responding to what don Carlos had said. "Señor Sevilla, I thank you for your concern and warning. I am aware of the great danger that lies ahead. Be that as it may, I cannot turn back from this course because it is dangerous, when God has so clearly called me to it and arranged the circumstances for me to come to Ecuador. Yet neither do I intend to go unprepared into the jungle to find the Aucas. My plan is to first learn their language and as much about their culture as possible. To this end I was hoping that you might be able to help me. Perhaps you know of an Auca who has left the tribe and from whom I can learn as much of the Auca language as possible."

"I have warned you. That is all I can do. I cannot stop you from following your plan," don Carlos said, looking straight at Rachel. "As to your request, my house girl speaks Auca. Perhaps she can help you."

Don Carlos called his house girl out to the courtyard and explained that Rachel wanted her to speak Auca words so that she could learn them.

Delighted to finally meet someone who spoke the Auca language, Rachel began by asking the house girl to speak various words in Auca and then use the words in a sentence. The house girl spoke the words, and Rachel scribbled them down phonetically in a notebook. As Rachel worked away, Catherine listened carefully to the house girl's words. Catherine had learned the Quichua language while in Peru, and after a while she leaned over and whispered into Rachel's ear, "She is not speaking pure Auca. She is mixing Quichua words with it."

Rachel stopped immediately. She knew from her SIL training that it was impossible to learn a language from someone who kept mixing her native tongue with a newly acquired one. Disappointed, she turned to don Carlos. "Unfortunately we will not be able to use this girl, because she appears to be mixing Quichua and Auca words together.

Don Carlos looked surprised and impressed. "Your observation is very astute. Indeed she is Quichua. She was captured by the Aucas as a young girl and lived among them for many years, learning their language. But it is a long time now since she escaped. Perhaps you are right. She may have forgotten much of the language. She has no one to speak it with. However, if you want to learn the Auca language, I have four Aucas working for me at Hacienda Ila in the Oriente. I will be going back there in several days for an extended period of time, and you may come and stay with me there and learn the language from them, if that is what you have your heart set on."

Rachel didn't know what to say. This was more than she had hoped for—not one but four speakers of the Auca language. "I would very much like to take you up on your most generous offer, señor Sevilla," Rachel replied.

After leaving don Carlos's home, Rachel and Catherine climbed into another taxi and headed for the residence of Ecuador's president, Velasco Ibarra. As the taxi bumped along, Rachel thought about her conversation with don Carlos; it had exceeded her wildest hopes. She silently prayed that her contact with the four Auca girls at Hacienda Ila would somehow lead her to their tribe. But as she prayed, questions swirled in her head. Why had these Aucas left their tribe in the first place? Would the tribe welcome them back? And most important, would they be willing to trust Rachel and teach her their language? These were questions Rachel knew she could not answer. Instead she quoted a Bible verse to herself. "All things work together for good to those who love God and are called according to His purpose." As the taxi drove through the gates to the president's residence, Rachel told herself that indeed everything would work together for good.

As the taxi pulled to a halt in front of President Ibarra's house, Rachel quickly pulled out the hat she had concocted for the occasion. It consisted of the headdress Chief Tariri had given her as a farewell gift, to which she had sewn at the front a black veil. She placed the headdress on her head and arranged the veil and then climbed out of the taxi. Cameron Townsend and the other Wycliffe translators who were going to be officially presented to the president were already there, and Rachel and Catherine made their way over to where the group was standing.

Soon the official ceremony got under way. Uncle Cam made a few opening remarks and then proceeded to introduce each of the translators who would be working in Ecuador. "This is Rachel Saint," he said when it came Rachel's turn to meet President Ibarra. "She wants to go and translate the Bible for the Auca tribe."

As Rachel shook the president's hand, President Ibarra stared at her headdress. Rachel quickly explained that the headdress was from the Shapra Indians of Peru, among whom she had lived for some time. The president nodded, then asked, "You are going to work with the Aucas?"

"Yes," Rachel replied politely.

"I flew over their territory a while back. They threw spears at my plane. No white person has ever been able to live among them. Are you sure you really want to try, señorita?"

Rachel looked President Ibarra right in the eye and said, "Yes. I believe God will make a way for me to do that."

Once again the president nodded and then moved on. Rachel hoped that her words had not sounded rude. They had just tumbled out as she opened her mouth. But as forthright as her words were, Rachel had to admit that that was exactly how she felt about the situation.

On February 2, 1955, a month after her forty-first birthday, Rachel set out with Catherine to meet the four Auca girls at Hacienda Ila. A floatplane operated by Jungle Aviation and Radio Service (JAARS), the aviation wing of Wycliffe Bible Translators, ferried them there. As the plane droned its way across the Oriente, Rachel reflected on how grateful she was to have Catherine accompanying her. She knew that Catherine's call was not to the Aucas but to the Záparo Indians, who lived along the Pastaza River in both Peru and Ecuador. Since Western diseases had taken a terrible toll on the Záparos in Peru, reducing their population greatly, Catherine had decided to accompany Rachel in the hope of finding more Záparo Indians to work among in Ecuador. But until she was able to locate the Záparos, she was happy to assist Rachel in her research into the Auca language.

Finally the pilot banked to the right and lined up the aircraft for a landing. Moments later the plane's floats were gliding along the Anzu River, a tributary of the Rio Napo. The plane made its way to the riverbank, right to the front door of Hacienda Ila. Rachel and Catherine climbed out and retrieved their belongings from the plane as a group of people emerged from the hacienda to greet them. Soon don Carlos Sevilla, who had arrived at the place several days before, strode out of the hacienda to greet Rachel and Catherine. "Welcome to Hacienda Ila, señoritas," he said.

Don Carlos gave orders for his servants to carry the two missionaries' bags as he led Rachel and Catherine into the hacienda. Rachel had to admit that she had not known what to expect, and Hacienda Ila turned out to be more impressive than she had imagined. The two-story hacienda had many rooms and was built of large logs cut from the surrounding jungle. It was furnished with Spanish colonial furniture. Large oil paintings adorned the walls, and woven rugs covered the polished wooden floors. The hacienda was surrounded by a number of smaller buildings that served as housing for the workers and as guest quarters. One of the buildings was a kitchen, and another was a small school for the children of the workers. Beyond the hacienda and its outbuildings stretched cultivated fields. Rachel marveled at the amount of work that must have been involved in cutting the fields from the surrounding dense jungle. In the fields grew sugar cane, bananas, and yucca, as well as grass on which cows and horses grazed. The whole place reminded Rachel of a medieval castle with all its various enterprises.

Don Carlos showed Rachel and Catherine to a guest room on the second floor. The room was large and lit by oil lamps. The floor was polished to such a shine that Rachel could almost see her face in it, and the bed linen was crisp and clean.

After they had settled into their new home, Rachel and Catherine joined don Carlos and several members of his family for dinner, which they ate seated at a long, wooden table in straight-backed chairs. Following dinner they moved to the veranda that ran the length of the house. As they sat talking, don Carlos finally asked, "Would you like to meet the Auca girls now?"

"Very much," Rachel replied.

Moments later the four Auca women walked out onto the veranda. They were dressed in cotton skirts and blouses. A small boy clung to the skirt of one of the women. The Aucas, whose skin was a coffee color, had thick, straight, black hair. In the lobes of each woman's ears were large holes, where the women had once worn balsa wood plugs.

Don Carlos introduced the women to Rachel and Catherine. Catherine then began to ask the Auca women questions in Quichua, the language spoken by the other Indians working at the hacienda and which the women understood and spoke. After a few minutes Catherine told Rachel that two of the girls were Quichuas who had lived with the Aucas for many years and that they, along with the youngest

Auca girl, had all forgotten the language. Pointing to the woman with the small boy at her side, she concluded, "Only this girl—Dayuma is her name—can still speak the language."

Rachel felt her heart begin to pound with excitement. Finally she had found someone who could speak the Auca language. "Ask her if she will help us learn her language," she instructed Catherine.

Dayuma spoke a few words in Quichua. "Yes, she will," Catherine interpreted jubilantly.

Over the next few minutes, Rachel learned that Dayuma's son was three years old and his name was Sam. Rachel also learned another important piece of information about the Aucas. Dayuma explained that the Aucas called themselves *Waorani,* which means "the people," and that the word *Auca* was actually a Quichua word meaning "savage."

"I will use the word *Waorani* to describe your tribe in the future," Rachel promised.

Because Dayuma worked all day long on the plantation, she and Rachel could meet together only at night. So, in the evenings, slowly but surely Rachel began to compile a list of Waorani words. As she looked at the words, she soon realized that the Waorani language was nothing like the Candoshi language the Shapra Indians spoke, as she had originally thought it might be.

One night Dayuma explained to Rachel how the Waorani counted. The system was simple and straightforward, until you got to twenty. Beyond that number, the Waorani had no way of counting. According to Dayuma, a Waorani counted one, two,

two and one, two and two, and then he or she would say, "*onompo omaempoquiae*," meaning, "as many fingers as there are on one hand." If they wanted to say nine, they would say, "as many fingers as there are on one hand and two and two." However, with a number like nine, Dayuma explained that more often than not a person would put his or her hands together and say, "as many fingers as there are on two hands," because ten was so close to nine and was easier to say. To count beyond ten, a person would put both hands together and look down at his or her toes and say, "two and one," to indicate thirteen. Rachel found it an intriguing but logical system, though she wondered how the Waorani would get on if they ever took to wearing shoes.

As Rachel worked at learning the Waorani language from Dayuma at Hacienda Ila, Shell Mera was frustratingly close, less than twenty miles away. It took only a few minutes to cover the distance by air. In fact, Nate would regularly fly overhead and drop mail to Rachel and Catherine, but he could not land, because there was no airstrip and MAF did not operate a floatplane. So as soon as it was practical, Rachel decided to trek through the jungle to visit Nate and Marj, who by now had three children. Their latest addition was a towheaded son, whom they had named Philip, after Nate and Rachel's brother.

At Shell Mera, as usual, brother and sister had a lot to catch up on. Nate was his usual enthusiastic self. He told Rachel about how he had been able to further perfect his spiral-line technique and how he was busier than ever in the Oriente. In the seven years that he and Marj had been at Shell Mera, the number of missionaries serving in the area had risen from twelve to twenty-five. Nate was modest, but Rachel knew that the nine mission stations could not work together without her brother's Piper aircraft, his piloting skills, and five new airstrips that had been built.

In fact, Nate and Marj had become so busy tending to the scattered mission stations that MAF had decided to base another couple at Shell Mera to help them with the workload. Nate had built a house next door to Shell Merita, in which Johnny and Ruth Keenan and their twin boys now lived. And with another pilot came another plane, this time a yellow Piper Cruiser, which Nate now flew most of the time instead of the Pacer.

Nate seemed particularly enthusiastic about the last three missionaries who had arrived in the area. He called them the Brethren boys because they were all working under the auspices of the Plymouth Brethren Church. The three, Jim Elliot, Ed McCully, and Pete Fleming, were all college graduates, and they brought with them a contagious enthusiasm as they set up mission stations in small villages throughout the area. Jim had married since arriving in the Oriente, and his wife, Betty, was about to give birth any day. Ed's wife, Marilou, was about to give birth to their second child. And Pete had returned to the United States on furlough and gotten married. Now he and his new wife, Olive, were in Quito, where Olive was learning Spanish before moving into the Oriente. Nate explained how much he and Marj enjoyed the friendship of the Brethren boys and their wives.

Nate had other good news to relay as well. Rachel knew that her brother had worked hard to get a medical clinic up and running at Shell Mera so that patients would not have to be flown over the Andes to get medical care. Under the direction of Dr. Art Johnston, the clinic was flourishing, and that very month, with help from Jim Elliot, Nate had begun work on a large new building for the clinic.

Of course Rachel wanted to know from Nate all he had learned about the Aucas. The news was not encouraging. The Aucas' pattern of attacking outsiders was continuing. Nate told how he had been involved in the latest incident. Early one morning he had flown from Shell Mera to the town of Villano, where an Ecuadorian army base was situated. The government had asked Nate to fly some supplies in for the soldiers. After finishing unloading the Piper Cruiser, Nate was revving the engine for takeoff when two soldiers came running toward him waving their arms. Nate explained how he had turned off the engine and heard the soldiers yelling that two wounded Quichua Indians needing medical attention were coming up the jungle trail.

Soon a Quichua man appeared, carrying a woman with a spear protruding from her lower back. The woman's husband limped along behind, with two spear wounds to his chest, one in his hand, and another in his thigh. Only two words needed to be said: "Auca attack!"

Nate told Rachel that he had strapped the couple in his plane and flown them to get emergency medical treatment.

Rachel's heart skipped a beat. "Were they able to tell you any more about the Aucas?" she asked.

Nate shook his head. "Not much. They figured the attack was probably a revenge killing for a raid on an Auca village years before, but they weren't sure. They pretty much agreed with everyone else that the Aucas are an unpredictable bunch. One thing seems certain though: everyone wants some kind of revenge. The Quichua man who was wounded tried to pay one of our workers to fly back into the area and kill at least one of the Aucas for him. Our worker tried to explain that we are not interested in killing other people but want to save them through faith in the Lord Jesus. The man didn't seem to understand that concept at all."

Rachel sat quietly for a moment. Then she said, "You know, Nate, I don't know how it's going to happen, but I believe that God is going to use my contact with Dayuma to crack that tribe wide open, and I will be the first person to go in and live among them."

Now it was Nate's time for silence. He slipped his arm through Rachel's, and the two of them sat peering through the window of Shell Merita, watching the sun set over Mount Sangay.

When Rachel returned to Hacienda Ila, she worked harder than ever to learn the Waorani language. Soon she was able to hold simple conversations with Dayuma. And what she learned from Dayuma about her tribe confirmed Nate's idea that the Waorani were caught in a brutal cycle of revenge killings. Rachel's first inkling of this came the evening Dayuma told her about her childhood.

Chapter 7

Dayuma's Story

One evening Rachel waited an extra long time for Dayuma to come in from the fields. When Dayuma finally arrived, she was in a particularly talkative mood. She sat down cross-legged on the floor of Rachel's room and began to talk. "Tonight I will tell you why I came to the outsiders."

Rachel grabbed her pencil and paper and sat beside Dayuma on a low stool. The oil lamp flickered as she started to write down what she heard from Dayuma. Although Rachel could not understand every word, she understood most of what Dayuma was trying to tell her.

"It was nine seasons ago of the kapok tree bursting forth when I lived at home with my people. Returning from hunting in the forest one day, my father Tyaento told us that he had a curse on him. He had fired his blowgun at a monkey but had not killed it. That is how he knew the spirits of the forest were angry with him. 'Now our enemy Moipa [a renowned killer in the tribe] will spear me, and I will die,' he told me. I was only fifteen seasons old and very afraid when I heard his words.

"The next dawn my father went into the forest, and he did not return that night, or for the next four nights. I was very afraid that Moipa had speared him, and I thought to myself, *Oh, when will my father come home?* Then I worried more. *What if Moipa had killed my father? Who will protect my mother and my younger sisters and brothers from his spear?* There was no one. So I gathered some friends and convinced them to come to the outside with me. They told me, 'The *cowadi* will kill you and eat you.' But I said, 'We shall see. It is better to run than to be killed by Moipa and lie unburied in the forest, isn't it?' So they came with me, and I said, 'Let's go! Hurry! We must pole faster than Moipa down the Curaray.'"

Rachel stopped Dayuma and asked her to explain the meaning of a couple of words, particularly *cowadi.* She learned that cowadi was the Waorani word for outsiders. After she had explained the meaning of the words to Rachel, Dayuma went on with her story.

"After two days we heard a noise in the jungle. We were very still, thinking it was Moipa, but it was not. It was my cousin Dawa running with her baby on her back. We stopped her, and she told us that Moipa had attacked our family. About twenty of our relatives had been speared in one night. Moipa had hacked my young sister to death with his machete."

Dayuma's voice broke as she spoke these words and then grew quieter as she continued.

"I asked about my mother, Akawo, but Dawa could not remember seeing her, and so I did not know if she was alive or dead. I could not go on knowing about my sister and wondering what could have happened to Akawo, so we turned around and poled our way back upriver. We went silently, and after three days I saw my mother's footprints on a beach."

Rachel nodded. She knew from her time living with Chief Tariri and the Shapra Indians that the natives of the Amazon jungle could read each other's footprints like signatures.

Dayuma shifted her weight and went on. "I followed the footprints into the jungle and there found my mother. 'Come with us, mother,' I begged. 'Let us go to the house of the cowadi and live. If we stay here, we will surely die.' 'No, my daughter,' Akawo replied. 'I will not be eaten by the cowadi. Don't they kill everyone who goes to them?' 'I don't know,' I told her, 'but peacefully I will go and see what becomes of me.'

"That was the last time I saw my mother," Dayuma said, her voice choking with emotion. "This time my cousin Umi, who had been with my mother, and two Quichua Indian girls who were slaves in my tribe decided to come with me. They had lived with our people for six years and were willing to go to the outside once again. Finally we found our way to don Carlos Sevilla's hacienda, and he gave us clothes and sent us to work in the fields."

"Have you heard anything about your family since you left?" Rachel asked, putting down her pencil.

Dayuma shook her head. "Nothing. No one else has come out to the cowadi. I do not know if it is because they are all dead or because they are afraid to come and look for us."

Rachel laid her hand on Dayuma's. "One day, maybe, you might go back to see if your mother is alive," she said.

Dayuma recoiled. "I will not return to be killed," she said. "I am an outsider now. Spearing me would make them happy."

"Perhaps God will tell us to go together," Rachel said.

Dayuma looked up at Rachel, her eyes wild with fear. "If Moipa does not kill us, then the *winae* will," she said.

"The winae? Who are the winae? Another tribe?" Rachel asked.

Dayuma looked toward the door as if she expected someone to walk through it. "The winae live in the jungle. They are little devils who come into our huts at night and suck the blood from us and kill us. My grandfather named for me once many in our family who had been killed by winae."

Rachel did not say anything. She wished that she could translate the Bible into Waorani faster than it was obviously going to take so that Dayuma could understand that God was stronger than any winae.

As the weeks turned into months, Rachel continued to learn more and more Waorani words from Dayuma. During the day while Dayuma worked in the fields, Rachel would write copious notes on what she had learned about the Waorani language and culture.

During this time Rachel received a letter from Doris Cox. Tears of joy streamed down her face as she read the letter, which recounted how Chief Tariri had finally become a Christian and given up his old ways. Then the chief's oldest son, Tsirimpo, had also become a Christian, followed by Tariri's wife, Irina, and then six other members of his family. Now Chief Tariri was busy urging other members in the tribe to accept the gospel, and he had witnessed to several other chiefs in the area.

After reading the letter, Rachel decided to show some photos of her and Chief Tariri to Dayuma. When she saw them, Dayuma was fascinated to see Rachel standing with a native family. After studying the photographs for several minutes, she said that she now believed that Rachel had lived with the Shapras and was serious about going to live with the Waorani.

Dayuma then explained to Rachel more about her tribal background. She described how Umi had seen Dayuma's father die before she fled the jungle, or, more precisely, how she had heard him die. According to Umi, Tyaento was speared by Moipa in the raid and badly wounded.

As she listened, Rachel soon learned that a Waorani's greatest fear is to be left alone in the jungle to die and rot. This fear is so deep that a Waorani would rather be buried alive than risk not being buried at all. And as Dayuma reported to Rachel, that is what had happened to her father. When the pain from the spear wounds had become too unbearable, Tyaento said to his brother, "Dig a hole for me so I can enter it. Cover me over and I will die." And that is what his brother did. In the traditional fashion, before covering the hole with dirt, he laid bamboo slats across it to create a breathing space. Umi had described to Dayuma how she had listened as Tyaento moaned and groaned while buried in the hole until the air in the breathing space finally ran out and he died.

Rachel felt sad for Dayuma after hearing the story. No wonder Dayuma did not want to go back to her people. Her father and sister were dead, and by now her mother probably was as well. The entire tribe was caught up in a cycle of violent, senseless killing, and Dayuma had every reason to believe that she would be the next one killed if she went back among the Waorani.

After accompanying Rachel to Hacienda Ila, Catherine Peeke had set out in search of Záparo Indians, leaving Rachel to plod on alone learning the Waorani language. Occasionally, though, another missionary would stop by Hacienda Ila, and Rachel was always grateful to have someone to talk and pray with.

One day at the end of October, Jim Elliot showed up. He had walked over from Shandia, a four-hour trek through the jungle. Since he and his wife, Betty, had also been through the Summer Institute of Linguistics in Oklahoma, Jim was interested in how Rachel was getting on learning the Waorani language. Rachel told him about spending her evenings with Dayuma, learning Waorani words and trying to understand their culture. Jim, in turn, reported to Rachel how things were progressing at Shandia. He explained that he had come to Hacienda Ila for two reasons: to buy two piglets from don Carlos and to meet Dayuma and have her translate several short sentences into the Waorani language for him. Dayuma happily obliged, and by midafternoon Jim had his two piglets and the translated sentences and had set off for Shandia so that he would make it home before sunset. After Jim, who was one of the Brethren boys, had left, Rachel had to admit that Nate was right: Jim Elliot did seem to have a contagious enthusiasm for his mission work in the Oriente.

As Christmas approached, Rachel decided that she had learned enough of the Waorani language to tell Dayuma the Christmas story in her own language. In preparation she wrote the story out in Waorani and read it word for word to Dayuma. When Rachel had finished reading, Dayuma sat and seemed to have no reaction to the story. Rachel's spirits sank at this reaction. It was not what she had expected. They both sat in silence for a long time before Dayuma finally spoke.

"Did all the angels sing what the first one said?" Dayuma asked.

Rachel breathed a sigh of relief. Dayuma had taken in the story after all and had carefully thought about it.

By Christmas Rachel needed a break, and she was happy to accept an invitation to spend a week with Nate and Marj at Shell Mera. Their time together was joyful. Shell Merita was decked out with Christmas decorations and strings of lights. In the corner of the living room was a small, artificial Christmas tree with wrapped presents underneath. Early on Christmas morning Kathy and Steve prodded one-year-old Phil awake and then dragged their parents and Aunt Rachel out of bed so that they could open their presents. As she watched the children tearing the wrapping paper off their gifts, Rachel thought how fortunate she was to have traveled so many miles from Pennsylvania yet still have family less than a day's walk away.

Rachel was still at Shell Mera on New Year's Day 1956. She spent some time that day reflecting on what lay ahead for her as she tried to reach the Waorani with the gospel. Indeed she had more questions than answers about what the coming year held for her. As she thought about the year ahead, she prayed, "Lord, I don't know what the future holds. Reach the tribe with or without me, but reach the tribe."

Rachel had no idea as she prayed these words that the next few days would change the course of not only her life but also the lives of countless other people.

Chapter 8

Tragedy

It was Rachel's forty-second birthday, January 2, 1956. She was sitting beside her brother in the passenger seat of the yellow Piper Cruiser. Nate was flying to Shandia to drop Rachel off and pick up Jim Elliot. Jim was on his way to run a week-long series of evangelical meetings at Arajuno. As a result Betty Elliot had asked Rachel if she would come to Shandia to help with the mission work there and look after one-year-old Valerie while Jim was away. Rachel had agreed to go, glad of the opportunity to finally see firsthand all that was going on in Shandia. Things there had sounded very exciting when she had talked to Jim two months before at Hacienda Ila. And while she was at Shell Mera for Christmas, Nate had told her that Jim had recently baptized twenty-five Quichua Indians and that the nucleus of a strong local church was forming. It all gave Rachel hope that one day she would be able to report similar progress among the Waorani.

The twenty-minute flight from Shell Mera to Shandia was uneventful. The Elliot family was waiting beside the airstrip as Nate brought the plane in for a landing. After an exchange of hellos and goodbyes, Nate was soon on his way again, with Jim as his passenger. Rachel, Betty, and Valerie stood near a grove of bamboo and watched the Piper Cruiser disappear from view over the jungle. As they turned and walked the short distance to the Elliots' house, Betty seemed a little distracted, and Rachel left her to her thoughts.

Once at the house, the two women shared a pot of coffee as Betty filled Rachel in on what needed to be done. Betty told Rachel that they had just completed a new schoolhouse and asked if she would be able to help teach the growing number of students of all ages who showed up each morning to learn to read and write.

Everything went according to plan. Rachel had plenty to do, and the week seemed to whiz by. By Monday morning, when Rachel was scheduled to leave, she was looking forward to returning to her language-learning work with Dayuma. All she was waiting for was a radio message from Marj to say that Nate was on his way to Shandia to pick her up. But as the morning dragged on, the radio remained strangely silent. There was no message from Marj.

Finally Rachel heard Betty call Marj on the radio in the next room. Rachel got up and walked over to the room. She hesitated for a moment in the doorway. She could hear the strain in her sister-in-law's voice. "Johnny has found the plane on the beach. All of the fabric is stripped off. There is no sign of the men," she heard Marj say.

The hairs on the back of Rachel's neck stood straight up, and one word sprung to her mind—*Aucas*. Without hearing another word, Rachel knew that her brother had somehow come in contact with them.

Betty turned to see Rachel in the doorway. "I have to go, Marj. Rachel is here. Can Johnny come and get us? I think we should all be together right now. Over," she said into the mouthpiece.

"I was thinking the same thing," Marj replied. "I'll radio you back when he's in the air. Over and out."

"I'm sorry. I didn't want you to have to find out this way," Betty said, turning to look Rachel in the eye, "but the men are in trouble. We've lost radio contact with them, and it doesn't look good."

A million questions raced through Rachel's mind, and over the next hour some of them were answered. It turned out, according to Betty, that Jim had hoped to reach the Aucas with the gospel since his days at Bible college. Jim had convinced his two fellow Brethren missionaries, Ed McCully and Pete Fleming, to help him find a way to do so. But no one could think of a safe way to go about making contact with them until Nate started telling them about the spiral-line technique he had developed.

As Rachel heard about this, her heart dropped. She recalled how proud Nate had been as he described the technique to her. Now it looked as though the spiral-line technique had played a central part in a plan that had gone very wrong.

Betty packed an overnight bag for her and Valerie and then told Rachel how things had developed. In mid-September Nate and Ed had flown over a group of Aucas, whom they dubbed the "neighbors," since the McCullys lived at Arajuno, right on the edge of Auca territory. Now that they had a location where a group of Aucas lived and a way to pass things down to them on the ground, they decided it would be a great opportunity to show the Aucas that the missionaries wanted to be their friends.

Over the next thirteen weeks, Nate and the other men made a once-a-week drop to the Auca village. Sometimes they put a machete in the bucket, and at other times they included clothes or small articles such as mirrors and sugar cubes. From all accounts, things were going well, and so Nate, the three Brethren missionaries, and Roger Youderian, who served with the Gospel Missionary Union at nearby Macuma, had decided to venture into Auca territory.

Rachel was stunned as she listened to what Betty was telling her. She felt betrayed, especially since Nate and Jim had been involved in the planning for over three months and that she had been misled into thinking that Jim was holding meetings at Arajuno.

She hardly trusted herself to speak as Betty caught her up on the last phase of the plan.

"There was a stretch of beach on the Curaray River, just four and a half miles from the Auca village. We called it 'Palm Beach,' and Nate said it was long enough to land the Piper on. So last week he ferried the men in to the site. The idea was for three of them to camp there while Nate and Pete flew in and out from Arajuno each day. Jim and the others assembled a prefabricated tree house in a large tree at the end of the beach and waited for the Aucas to pay them a visit. And two Auca women and a man did come and visit them. The men gave them gifts, and Nate even took the Auca man up for a flight in the plane. Things were looking promising. But last night, while you were out at Bible study, Marj radioed to say that Nate hadn't flown out from Palm Beach back to Arajuno before dark as usual. So at first light this morning, Johnny Keenan flew over Palm Beach to take a look. And you heard what he found. The Piper Cruiser has been stripped of its fabric skin, and there is no sign of the men."

As Rachel heard more details of the plan, her emotions raged within her. Fear, frustration, disbelief, and anger coursed through her as she thought about what the men had done. But her thoughts were interrupted by the sound of an airplane buzzing the house. For a brief moment her heart skipped a beat. Was it Nate telling them he was safe? Then she remembered that Nate's little yellow airplane lay stripped on Palm Beach. Rachel ran to the doorway anyway, just in time to see Johnny Keenan in the Piper Pacer circle the house one more time and then head for the airstrip.

The two women walked silently along the path that led to the airstrip. Betty carried Valerie on her hip while Rachel carried the bags. Once they reached the airstrip, one look at Johnny's face told Rachel that Johnny had no good news to report. The atmosphere inside the plane was tense and silent as Johnny flew them to Shell Mera. As soon as Rachel, Betty, and Valerie had climbed out of the Pacer, Johnny took to the air again to go and collect Marilou McCully, Olive Fleming, and Barbara Youderian.

As Rachel walked toward Shell Merita, she saw her niece Kathy and remembered that today was Kathy's seventh birthday. But Kathy barely smiled when Rachel wished her a happy birthday.

Rachel walked inside the house, and Marj got up from the radio console and hugged her. "I am so sorry you didn't know," she said. "This must be a terrible shock to you."

"Yes, it is," Rachel replied, not really wanting to talk about her feelings.

Just as in the airplane on the way from Shandia to Shell Mera, a tense silence pervaded Shell Merita.

As Rachel, lost in a confusion of thought, sat staring blankly at Mount Sangay in the distance, there was a knock at the door. Marj opened the door, and there stood Larry Montgomery, a pilot for Wycliffe Bible Translators. Larry greeted Marj and quickly explained that he had been passing through Quito when he had the strangest feeling he should get on a bus and make the thirteen-hour trip to Shell Mera. He apologized for not letting Marj know ahead of time that he was coming.

"Come in and sit down, Larry," Marj said calmly. "I have something to tell you."

Soon Marj was telling Larry the details of Operation Auca, as the men had named it. Larry listened carefully to everything Marj told him, and when she was finished, he sprang into action, taking charge of the situation. Larry, as it turned out, was a friend of General Harrison, the man in command of the U.S. military for the whole Caribbean region. General Harrison was a Christian, and Larry was sure that if he could get ahold of the general by shortwave radio, the general would help. Rachel watched as Marj led Larry to the radio room, where he sent out a message. Within half an hour General Harrison was on the radio. Larry described the situation to the general and asked if the military could help. General Harrison promised he would do all he could.

An hour later another radio transmission confirmed that help was on the way. General Harrison had called Air Force Major Nurnberg in Panama and ordered him to head up a military rescue team, which by now was winging its way from Panama toward Shell Mera.

As Rachel listened to the news that a rescue team was on the way, she felt herself becoming calmer.

No matter how they had arrived at this point, now was the time to be clearheaded and do whatever she could to ensure the men's survival.

After the sun set that night, Rachel found herself alone with Marj. It was a painful moment.

"Why didn't they tell me?" Rachel asked softly. "I could have helped them with the language and added my prayers to theirs."

Marj nodded and disappeared into the bedroom. She emerged a minute later holding an envelope, which she gave to Rachel. The writing on the front said, "To be held until further notice." Rachel opened the envelope and began to read.

> Dear Sis,
>
> As you know, the reaching of the Aucas has been on our hearts for a long time. It has been heartening to know that the Lord has laid a specific burden on your heart also and that you are currently engaged in work on their language.

Rachel stopped reading for a moment to wipe her eyes. Then she read on.

> For this reason it has been hard to decide not to share with you the efforts that we are about to initiate toward the contacting of these people. Our efforts will be directed toward inspiring confidence in Ed McCully, who is,

> as you know, living within easy reach of the Aucas in two days overland.
>
> I am writing this note now so that you will better understand and so that I will be spared an embarrassed effort to explain it to you after the need for secrecy blows over.

Rachel turned the page and continued,

> As we see it, you might feel obligated to divulge this information to save me the risks involved. In view of that fact, and since we know that you are already praying for the contacting of these people, we trust God to carry us forward in this effort and you in your effort to the end that Christ might be known among them.
>
> Affectionately, Nate

Over the next two days as news of the disappearance of the five missionaries filtered out to the world, airplanes began swooping down on the Shell Mera airstrip, bringing in all manner of people. Rachel's oldest brother, Sam, arrived to add his support, as did two representatives from Christian Missions in Many Lands, the Plymouth Brethren mission agency under which Jim Elliot, Pete Fleming, and Ed McCully served. MAF president Grady Parrott also made his way to Shell Mera from Los Angeles. And Abe Van Der Puy, a missionary in Quito with HCJB radio, came to coordinate the sending out of news bulletins and press releases. Jerry Hannifin, foreign correspondent for *Time* magazine, also made his way from Quito to the Oriente, and in Washington, D.C., famous *Life* magazine photographer Cornell Capa convinced his superiors to let him cover the story, and he too made his way to Shell Mera.

Equipment arrived also. By Tuesday night two Air Force C-47 cargo planes had arrived from Panama. One carried a rescue team, and the other an H-13 helicopter. The following morning the helicopter was unloaded and quickly assembled for use in the search. Ecuadorian Air Force planes that had ferried in twenty soldiers were there also to help with the search.

Rachel tried to help in any way she could, but she also tried to stay out of the way of all the busy people around her. No bodies had been sighted, and people clung to the hope that somewhere out in the jungle the men might still be alive. But deep in her heart Rachel feared the worst. Knowing what she now knew about the Waorani, she was aware that if the Waorani discovered the five men in their territory, they would surely kill them.

In case the men were still alive and trying to escape from Auca territory through the jungle, a search party was hastily organized. Frank Drown, who worked with Roger and Barbara Youderian at Macuma, asked to lead it. He had worked in the Oriente for twelve years and knew better than anyone what the crew would be up against trying to make it overland to Palm Beach. Dr. Art Johnston from the medical clinic volunteered to join the search party, as did several other missionaries in the area. They gathered at Arajuno and set out at first light on Wednesday morning, January 11, accompanied by thirteen Ecuadorian soldiers.

Wednesday also brought the news Rachel feared. Johnny Keenan had flown over Palm Beach again, and this time he had spotted two bodies floating in the river about a quarter of a mile downstream. Both bodies were clad in khaki pants and white T-shirts. Since any of the men in the group could have been wearing those clothes, Johnny could not tell whose bodies they were.

By Thursday the helicopter was up and running, and it flew out to Palm Beach to search for the men. When it returned to Shell Mera, Major Nurnberg, commander of the U.S. Air Force search team, reported that the team had sighted four partially submerged bodies in the vicinity of Palm Beach.

On Friday morning Rachel watched the helicopter take off once again and head out across the jungle. She learned that the ground party had made it safely to Palm Beach and the helicopter was going to help the men on the ground locate the bodies. Rachel, along with Marj and the wives of the other four men, waited patiently for the ground party to return and report what they had found.

Two and a half days later the ground party made it back to Shell Mera. Soon after their arrival Rachel and the five wives gathered in the kitchen of Shell

Merita to hear Art Johnston describe what they had found at Palm Beach.

Art reported that Thursday, January 12, 1956, was a day the men in the search party would never be able to forget, no matter how hard they tried. The men spent the first night camped outside Auca territory, and at dawn they broke camp and headed into dangerous territory. They poled their dugout canoes down the shallow, winding Curaray River, and about midmorning they met a group of Quichua Indians making their way upstream. This was a surprise, since the Indians were coming from deep in the heart of Auca territory. Frank Drown talked to them and learned that they were Christians from Arajuno, where Ed and Marilou McCully lived. When they heard of what had happened, they had put together their own search party to go after their missionary. But the news they related to Frank was not good. The Indians had found Ed's body downstream from the airplane. One of the Quichuas had Ed's watch with him to give to Marilou. The men had taken off one of Ed's shoes and carried it back upstream and left it beside the remains of the airplane.

Rachel listened intently as Art relayed how, after meeting the group of Quichuas, the hopes of the search team at finding any of the men alive began to fade. The team poled on downstream, keeping a sharp watch for any movement or sound in the jungle at the side of the river that might indicate that Auca killers were nearby.

Finally, as the skies darkened with rain, the search party arrived at Palm Beach. The U.S. military helicopter brought in from Panama swooped down near them, as planned. It headed downstream a few yards and hovered. The men knew that the helicopter was signaling where the first body was. They found the body caught in a tree branch and dragged it upstream. The helicopter moved on. Within an hour the search party had recovered the bodies of four men. The bodies had been in the water too long and were unrecognizable. But watches and wedding rings told the members of the search party who they were: the bodies of Nate Saint, Jim Elliot, Roger Youderian, and Pete Fleming.

Art reported that the body of Ed McCully was nowhere to be found. The members of the search party decided that the river must have washed it away. However, they did find the shoe beside the airplane, where the Quichuas said they had thrown it. And there was no question that it was Ed's. Ed had enormous feet and wore size thirteen and a half shoes. The shoe also confirmed that the Quichuas had indeed seen Ed's body. There was no doubt, reported Art, that all five of the men were dead.

Rachel sat in silence as Art went on to describe how Frank had climbed an ironwood tree to the tree house the men had built, hoping to find some clue as to what had happened to provoke the gruesome killings. But alas, Frank found none.

As the skies got blacker, the members of the search party worked nervously to dig a common grave under the ironwood tree. The thirteen Ecuadorian soldiers stood guard on the perimeter of Palm Beach, facing the jungle, their fingers at the ready on the triggers of their rifles, watching for the slightest movement of the leaves.

When the rain began to fall heavily, the search party pulled sheets of aluminum from the roof of the tree house and balanced them over their heads for shelter. There was a huge crack of thunder just as the bodies were being lowered into the common grave. Frank said a short prayer aloud over the bodies. As soon as the bodies were buried, the search party set out for home. They were worried about their own safety, and as they made their way mile by mile out of Auca territory, they were alert to the crack of even a twig in the jungle, fearing it might signal that a group of Aucas were preparing to attack and kill them.

Finally Art handed over the personal items the members of the search party had collected from the bodies. At the bottom of the river the men had also found Nate's camera, the undeveloped film still in it. Art laid the camera on the table in front of Marj.

After hearing the harrowing account of what the search party had found, Rachel knew it was time to write to her parents. She wrote:

> For you two, so far away, we pray the Holy Spirit's comforting. I told the Lord I was willing to make any sacrifice to reach these Indians—and this is the first thing He has asked of me. As you know, Nate was precious to me. We rejoice that he is in the Lord's presence now....

> May God yet give me the privilege of going to these same Indians and translating His precious Word for them and seeing the harvest from the five grains of wheat planted way down on the Curaray River in Auca soil.

Yes, her brother was dead, killed by the very people to whom she had devoted the rest of her life to reaching with the gospel, but Rachel would not look back or second-guess her calling. Something good would come from her brother's death. She had to believe that.

Chapter 9

Back to the Hacienda

Rachel and her new partner, Mary Sargent, marched along the jungle path in single file. It was March 1956, and Rachel was finally returning to Hacienda Ila. Huge air plants, some with leaves two to three feet wide, dangled from the tops of the trees above. Monkeys, calling to one another, played in the branches above; toucans squawked; and tree frogs croaked. Despite the constant backdrop of noise above them, the two women walked in silence on the jungle floor.

As Rachel walked, many questions popped into her head. Two months had passed since the killing of the five men, and Rachel wondered whether Dayuma would still be waiting at the hacienda for her return. She had heard rumors of news reporters offering Dayuma money to guide them back into Waorani territory. Had Dayuma done that? And how would the killing of the five men change Rachel and Dayuma's relationship? The photos developed from Nate's recovered camera showed the three Waoranis who had visited the men at Palm Beach before their deaths. These pictures had been printed in every newspaper in Ecuador. Rachel was sure that someone would have shown them to Dayuma. But what if one or more of the visitors were her relatives? Would that create a gulf between Rachel and Dayuma? And if one of them was a relative, was Dayuma so steeped in the Waorani pattern of killing and revenge that she would expect Rachel to kill her?

Rachel had no answers to these questions and instead tried to divert her thoughts by praying for the five widows and their children. In the two months since the killings, each of the wives had made a decision about what to do next. Marilou McCully, who was eight and a half months pregnant at the time of her husband's death, had returned immediately to Pontiac, Michigan, to have the baby. There, Rachel heard, she had given birth to a healthy son. Olive Fleming had stayed with Betty Elliot and her daughter Valerie at Shandia for a month before returning home to the United States, where she was in high demand as a speaker about the martyred men. Barbara Youderian and her two children were back at the mission station at Macuma, where Barbara divided her time between caring for the children and helping with various mission duties. And Marj Saint was still at Shell Mera, seated day after day in her familiar spot by the radio, only this time she was following the comings and goings of Johnny Keenan, not Nate. As soon as a replacement pilot arrived to take Nate's place, Marj intended to move to Quito and run the World Radio Missionary Fellowship (HCJB) guest house for missionaries.

It seemed, however painfully, that each of the wives was getting on with her life. The five widows were constantly in the spotlight, with reporters coming to ask questions and photograph them. Rachel, though, often seemed forgotten in all this media attention. In truth, she was grateful for this. It had allowed her to go quietly about helping Marj with the children and waiting for the right time to rejoin Dayuma. Now, with Mary Sargent at her side, Rachel felt that the time was right, and she was returning to her plodding job of unraveling the Waorani language.

Finally, as the late afternoon sun began to sink behind the Andes Mountains and shadows crept across the Oriente jungle, Rachel and Mary rounded the last bend in the track and saw Hacienda Ila in the distance. A few minutes later a woman came rushing out of the house and began running toward Rachel. It was Dayuma.

"You came back!" Dayuma yelled gleefully. "You didn't die. You came back!"

Soon Rachel and Dayuma were locked in an embrace, with young Sam clinging to Rachel's knees.

"You are here!" Dayuma exclaimed, standing back to take a good look at Rachel. "Sometimes I would go out alone and call to the sky 'Rachel! Come back!' and you did."

Rachel smiled. Any doubts she may have had about having a strained relationship with Dayuma as a result of the killings were erased.

Once Rachel had taken her backpack to her room and greeted don Carlos Sevilla, she sat down on the veranda with Dayuma. Their conversation turned quickly to the killings, as they were the reason Rachel had been away for so long.

As they talked, Rachel showed Dayuma color copies of the photographs developed from the film in Nate's camera. Dayuma was impressed with the quality and clarity of the photos compared to the grainy images she had seen printed in the local newspaper. She stared carefully at each of the photos, studying the faces of the people in them.

Finally, after several minutes of this, Dayuma exclaimed, "Aunt Mintaka!" Rachel said nothing as Dayuma pointed to the older Waorani woman in one of Nate's photos.

"She is my mother's sister," Dayuma explained. "And her," she said, pointing to the young girl in the picture, "I think she is my little sister Gimari. But I cannot be sure. She has changed much. And him," she added, pointing to the man the five missionaries at Palm Beach had nicknamed George, "I think he is a relative too."

Rachel explained that the three Waoranis in the picture had visited Palm Beach on the Friday before the men were speared to death and had spent the day with the missionaries.

Dayuma studied another photograph closely. It was of a number of gifts the Waoranis had placed in the basket at the bottom of the spiral line in exchange for the ones Nate had lowered to them. The sight of the gifts, especially the baskets and mats woven with unique Waorani designs, seemed to stir a deep longing in Dayuma for her people. "Who knows," Dayuma told Rachel wistfully. "If my aunt is alive, then perhaps my mother is still alive too."

As Rachel talked more with Dayuma about the killing of Nate and the four others, Dayuma would often interrupt her to say, "I am sorry that they killed your brother and the other good foreigners."

Each time Dayuma apologized, Rachel would remind her that God was in control and that one day, in His time, He would cause something good to come from the deaths of the men. "Besides," Rachel would add, "Nate might be gone, but I will see him again one day in heaven."

Dayuma was intrigued by the last statement, and she wanted to know how a body could come back to life after it was dead. Using the story of the raising of Lazarus from the dead by Jesus, Rachel carefully explained God's power to resurrect the dead and how after we die, our spirits go to be with God in heaven. That was where Nate's spirit had gone, she explained, and one day her spirit would go there also, and she and Nate would be reunited. It took a while, but Dayuma finally grasped the concept, and Rachel watched her face light up in delight.

Not long after Rachel arrived back at Hacienda Ila, don Carlos and many of his workers moved to Hacienda San Carlos farther along the Anzu River. Rachel knew that don Carlos had been building the new place for several years and that it was an even larger plantation than Hacienda Ila. Since Dayuma was moving to the new hacienda, don Carlos assumed that Rachel and Mary Sargent would also move to the new location. And that is what happened.

At first the move had a positive effect on Rachel's language work. Dayuma was promoted to house girl, giving her greater opportunity to spend time with Rachel during the day. But there were also new pressures on the language partnership, brought on by all the media attention the death of the five men at Palm Beach continued to generate.

After the killings, the widows had designated Betty Elliot to write an official account of the tragedy. The ensuing book, titled *Through Gates of Splendor*, went on sale in bookstores in August 1956. The book was an instant best seller. At the same time, *Reader's Digest* published an article about the killings that was widely read. Every day, it seemed, someone tried to contact Rachel or one of the five widows to learn more details about the killings and about the Aucas. In a letter to her parents, Rachel explained the difficulties this caused.

> The picture has changed considerably. A year ago we were the only ones taking an active step toward learning the Auca language, and now the whole world is interested. This has made it exceedingly difficult for me. I will appreciate your special prayers that the Lord will enable me to do my part

> quietly. I have no desire for publicity—but I do feel I should continue with Dayuma. I have a love for her and she for me, and the Lord knows my heart. Nate himself always hoped the way would be made for me to reach the tribe.

The prayers of Rachel's parents appeared to go unanswered, however. Hacienda San Carlos became a crossroads for adventurers, writers, and curiosity seekers, who all wanted, and in some cases demanded, Dayuma's attention. Some of them even suggested to don Carlos Sevilla that he contract Dayuma out to them as a guide. Rachel was very gratified by Dayuma's response to this. "When God tells me to go, I will go," she said.

Soon Rachel was hardly able to spend any time at all with Dayuma, and she wrote in her diary,

> Prayed for faith to continue without discouragement. Only the Lord can prosper the work while we're hearing the language for only about three hours a week—but He can, or He can change the circumstances.

In the meantime, everyone seemed to have a plan on how to reach the Aucas. MAF workers came to Rachel with the idea of sending Dayuma up in a small plane and using a loudspeaker to broadcast the gospel to her people. Rachel balked at this idea because she was not sure exactly what Dayuma might say in the excitement of the moment. Dayuma had a deep hatred for the men who had killed her family, and Rachel feared that she might use the opportunity to threaten them, thus destroying any hope of future trust between the Waorani and the missionaries.

Rachel was also concerned about taking the only fluent speaker of the Waorani language outside of the tribe and flying her over dangerous jungle terrain. It seemed to her, as she was sure Nate would have pointed out, to be an unacceptable risk.

Still, many people questioned Rachel's judgment in the matter, and Rachel was glad when she learned that Dr. Kenneth Pike, her linguistics teacher and director of SIL, was coming to visit. By now Ken had married Cam Townsend's niece and was a world-renowned linguistics expert.

When Ken arrived at Hacienda San Carlos, Rachel poured out all of her frustrations to him. Ken listened patiently and assured Rachel that she was doing the right thing. "Keep up the good fight," he encouraged. "Surely there will come a time when you will use this language to reach many people."

Rachel held on to these words, though at times her faith in them all but evaporated. Her hope of reaching the Waorani was stretched nearly to breaking point when she learned what had happened to Dr. Tidmarsh, an elderly Plymouth Brethren missionary whom Jim Elliot had replaced at Shandia. When he heard what had happened to his young replacement, Dr. Tidmarsh returned to the Oriente in the hope of carrying on the work of reaching the Waorani. He had been staying in a small cabin in their territory, spending the weekdays and weeknights there and the weekends at Arajuno. One Monday when he returned to his cabin in the jungle, he found the place in a shambles. Two crossed spears were in the doorway, and two more were thrust into the windows. One spearhead had several pages from the Bible on the end of it. Betty Elliot later identified the pages as coming from Jim's Bible. It was not a good sign, and Dr. Tidmarsh did not stay in the jungle.

When Rachel heard about the incident, she despaired at how anyone was going to get close enough to the Waorani so that they could see that their visitors meant them no harm.

Meanwhile, the work learning and understanding the Waorani language continued slowly. One break in the monotony came when don Carlos allowed Rachel to take Dayuma to Quito for Christmas. By now, Marj Saint was running the HCJB missionary guest house in the city, and she made the two women feel welcome.

Marj's three children were doing well. Kathy and Steve, the oldest two, were attending the Christian Missionary Alliance school at the end of the street.

Rachel enjoyed her time with Marj and the children, but most of all she loved to sit and watch Dayuma interact with the missionaries. It was the first time that Dayuma had been around a large group of Christians, and Rachel could tell that it was having quite an effect on her. Within days Dayuma was asking Rachel to tell her new Bible stories, and Dayuma's face shined as she listened to them.

By the time the two returned to Hacienda San Carlos, Rachel was convinced that Dayuma had understood the gospel and had accepted it. This conviction was borne out by Dayuma's eagerness to tell her young Waorani friend Winaemi the new Bible stories she had learned. Although the two young women spoke together in Quichua, Rachel understood much of what Dayuma said. When she had finished relaying one of the Bible stories, Dayuma turned to Rachel and said, "If you teach her about God, she will come to love Him. Now she loves Him just a little bit. I will tell her lots, and then she will come to love Him lots.... Why was I not caused to love Him long ago?"

Rachel thought of the missionaries who were waiting to reach Dayuma's people with the gospel as soon as they appeared ready to receive it—or at least would not kill them at first sight.

In April 1957 Rachel received a very strange request from Cameron Townsend. At first she dismissed the request outright, saying it was too outrageous to consider. But as she prayed about it, Rachel came to believe that God wanted her and Dayuma to comply with Uncle Cam's request. By June the two women were on their way to Hollywood, California!

Chapter 10

Surprises

It was June 1, 1957, one year and five months since the five men had been speared to death at Palm Beach. Rachel was sitting in a large commercial airliner with Dayuma at her side, clutching her hand. The plane was circling Miami International Airport, preparing to land. This was their first stop in the United States. After they had cleared customs and immigration in Miami, they would board another airplane for the final leg of their journey to California.

Rachel had been asked to bring Dayuma to the United States to take part in a television show about don Carlos Sevilla, to be titled *The Daniel Boone of Ecuador*. Cameron Townsend was eager for Dayuma to appear on the show. He had written to Rachel in Ecuador, explaining how important Dayuma's appearance on the show could be in spreading the word about what Wycliffe Bible Translators was doing in the Oriente. And although that was not the focus of the show, Uncle Cam hoped that in the course of being interviewed about don Carlos, Dayuma might say something to publicize the mission's work.

At first Uncle Cam's argument had not swayed Rachel as she contemplated the enormous culture shock involved in bringing a Waorani woman to the United States as well as the possibility of Dayuma's dying from a Western disease to which she had no immunity. But in the end Rachel decided to go along with Uncle Cam's request, recognizing that he was the leader of her mission. And now Rachel and Dayuma were en route to Hollywood.

Finally the plane landed in Miami, where the women deplaned and where Dayuma's cross-cultural education began. Rachel watched Dayuma's eyes get as big as saucers at the sight of so many white faces. When they stopped to buy a snack, Dayuma did not know what to make of all the food choices arrayed before her. And when she did finally choose some potato chips, she complained to Rachel that they were much too spicy. As they sat eating, Dayuma looked around at the crowds of people coming from and going to airplanes and asked, "Rachel, do all of these people love God?"

Rachel took a deep breath and wondered how to tell Dayuma that all of these people had access to the Bible but very few of them read it or lived by it.

After their stopover in Miami, Rachel and Dayuma were soon in the air, winging their way toward Hollywood.

On Wednesday evening, June 5, Rachel took Dayuma to rehearse for the television show about don Carlos Sevilla. As she sat on a platform decorated with palms and a thatched hut, Rachel chatted with Ralph Edwards, who would be hosting the show. As she sat talking, she heard the unmistakable voice of her father from off stage. Rachel was surprised and confused that the producers of the show had gone to the trouble of making a tape recording of her father for her. Then out of the corner of her eye she saw someone approaching the stage. Rachel turned to look—it was her father!

"What are you doing here?" Rachel asked as she rushed to hug her father. Just then her brother Sam stepped onto the set, followed by several old school friends from Huntingdon Valley. By now Rachel was too shocked to move. As Sam walked up and kissed her, he whispered into her ear, "Don't make it hard for Ralph, Sis. He's working against time."

In an electrifying second, Rachel realized what was happening. She was the subject of the show, and it was not a rehearsal at all. The cameramen were filming the show and broadcasting it live! At the same moment Ralph Edwards, with a huge grin on his face, looked into the camera and announced, "Rachel Saint—this is your life."

Since she had spent the last several years living in Peru and Ecuador, Rachel did not realize that *This Is Your Life* was a hugely popular television show in the United States. Each week an unsuspecting celebrity or interesting person was lured by some ruse to the studio, where the person was surprised with the news that he or she was the featured guest. On the show, one by one, people significant in the guest's life were brought out to offer anecdotes about the person. And with the ruse about filming a show on don Carlos Sevilla, Rachel had been lured onto the show, which thirty million people were now watching live.

Barely able to comprehend what was happening to her, Rachel tried her best to explain the unfolding events to Dayuma as a stream of people were brought onstage. There were her childhood friend Beryl Walsh Adcock from Huntingdon Valley, her parents and brothers, Dr. Addison Raws from the Keswick Colony of Mercy, and Loretta Anderson from the Shapra tribe in Peru. The only person Rachel was not surprised to see was don Carlos Sevilla, as she had expected him to show up sometime during the "rehearsal interview."

Just when Rachel thought things could not get any more bizarre, she heard the unmistakable voice of a Shapra Indian. She recognized it immediately as the voice of Chief Tariri. Moments later, followed by his wife, Irina, and his youngest son, Tariri was bounding across the stage toward Rachel. He was wearing his chiefly regalia, complete with feathered headdress, beads, and beetle-wing earrings. He greeted his "sister" Rachel with a kiss.

"Tiyotari [Rachel] wrote paper day after day," Chief Tariri said. "She told us, 'In God's house you will live well. If you obey Jesus, then you will be good.' In my heart I thought, 'You are telling the truth.' I began to love Jesus. Who else is like Him? What person can do the things He did?"

After the filming and broadcasting of the thirty-minute show, the entire "cast" moved to the Hollywood Roosevelt Hotel, where Rachel and Dayuma were staying. Rachel laughed to herself as they all walked through the lobby; they were an odd-looking group. She assumed that the staring hotel guests would think that Tariri was dressed in some kind of movie costume. No one would suspect that he was an ex-headhunting chief from the Peruvian jungle.

Rachel's friends and family stayed at the hotel for the next two days, which proved to be two of the best days of Rachel's life. Rachel told everyone that she had never expected that such a group of people so dear to her would ever meet each other this side of heaven. The guests were served their meals in their rooms so that they could avoid the public eye and be allowed to talk freely together. A worker with Wycliffe Bible Translators in Los Angeles even arranged to keep the disoriented Indian visitors supplied with chicken and boiled rice.

During this time Chief Tariri and Dayuma tried to communicate, though it was not easy because of the language gulf that existed between them. Except for the translation of a few simple phrases by the Wycliffe missionaries present, most of Tariri and Dayuma's communication was through smiles and gestures. Still, Chief Tariri seemed genuinely pleased with the meeting. "Tiyotari," he told Rachel, "it is good to meet one of the Aucas that God has sent you to. I can see with my eyes that they also need the same message you brought to us."

It took Rachel several days to recover from the shock of being thrust onto the *This Is Your Life* show. It took her even longer to adjust to the idea that Uncle Cam and the Wycliffe Bible Translators had a full year's agenda planned for her and Dayuma in the United States. Both Rachel and Dayuma wanted to return to Ecuador, but once again Rachel found herself outmaneuvered by the powers above her.

From California Rachel and Dayuma traveled to the University of Oklahoma, where another Summer Institute of Linguistics was under way. When they arrived there, Dayuma obligingly allowed the would-be linguists to interview her and try out their new language acquisition skills on her. As well, Rachel received help with some difficult Waorani language concepts from her mentor Ken Pike.

Sometimes Rachel despaired that Dayuma did not grasp the gospel message at all, but she saw some encouraging signs along the way. While in Oklahoma, Rachel explained to Dayuma how to pray a simple prayer, but Dayuma seemed reluctant to say anything. In response Rachel wrote down a simple prayer in Waorani and read it aloud. When Dayuma heard it, she shook her head disapprovingly. "We don't talk like that in our language," she said.

Rachel scanned the text for the grammatical error she was sure Dayuma was referring to. "Tell me what mistake I made," she said.

Dayuma's response was short. "It's not the words you said. We just don't talk to God in our language."

Now Rachel understood. Dayuma had never heard anyone pray in Waorani, and she assumed that to pray she would have to use Quichua or learn English. It took some convincing before Dayuma felt comfortable praying in her native language.

On June 15, Rachel and Dayuma flew to New York City to speak at a Billy Graham Evangelical Crusade in progress at Madison Square Garden. A crowd of over sixteen thousand had packed into the building, and Rachel was concerned about how Dayuma would react when placed in front of such a big crowd. After all, until recently Dayuma had no idea that there were that many people in the rest of the world.

Much to Rachel's relief, Dayuma seemed to take addressing the huge crowd in stride. She was a little shy at first, but then she started recounting one of the Bible stories Rachel had told her. It was the one about how Jesus raised Jairus's daughter from the dead. Rachel translated Dayuma's version of the story into English, delighted by how the crowd was enraptured at the simple storytelling of a tribal woman. When Dayuma ended with the thought that Jairus's parents were very, very happy, the crowd cheered. Later, when there was a call for people to go forward who wanted to become Christians, hundreds of people headed toward the front. Dayuma was astounded that so many people did not follow "God's Carvings" (the Bible) in a land where they were so accessible.

While staying in Manhattan for the crusade, Rachel realized that Dayuma had no way to comprehend many of the things she saw. The skyscrapers and the Statue of Liberty did not seem to impress Dayuma. What fascinated her were the window cleaners dangling from the Empire State Building. How did they get there? she wanted to know. And why don't they fall?

From New York the pair traveled on to Philadelphia, where Rachel visited her parents. Rachel was gratified to see that her mother and Dayuma got along very well. Despite the language barrier, the two women seemed to understand each other. Dayuma was well aware that Nate was Mrs. Saint's son. She told Rachel later that she had looked for any signs of bitterness in her mother over the death of Nate and was astounded to find none. Now she believed Rachel when she said that she did not want to make contact with the Waorani to avenge the death of her brother Nate.

As Rachel thought about the rapport between her mother and Dayuma, she realized that Dayuma had been around very few older people. In the jungle, almost every adult Dayuma knew had been speared to death by early middle age. Rachel understood that seeing old people living well and without fear of death was a tremendous encouragement to Dayuma.

Rachel enjoyed the time at home with her parents, but it had become a strain for Rachel and Dayuma to be anywhere outside the confines of the family home. Following the *This Is Your Life* show, Rachel and Dayuma had become quite famous, and strangers would stop them in the street to engage them in conversation or ask for an autograph. After a while the constant attention became very tiring, and everyone decided that it would be best to rent a quiet cabin for a month in the pine forests of Pennsylvania. As it turned out, this was a wonderful decision. For the first time since arriving in the United States, Rachel was able to relax. And Dayuma seemed to be more at home in the forest, although at times she had flashbacks to her childhood and became very scared.

As the weeks went by, Rachel could see that Dayuma still had many old fears. Dayuma believed, for instance, as did the Waorani, that mosquitoes possessed evil spirits, which they passed on to anyone they bit. To Dayuma the forest seemed infested with devils that could pounce upon a person and suck the lifeblood from them. The situation saddened Rachel and drove her to pray harder than ever that Dayuma would understand the power of God to overcome such fears.

In September, Rachel and Dayuma attended the Wycliffe Bible Translators' biennial meeting in the tiny town of Sulphur Springs, Arkansas, where Rachel met with many of the Wycliffe workers she had known through the years. It was a joyous reunion, until Dayuma came down with the Asian flu. Her temperature soared, and every bone and muscle in her body ached. Rachel grew desperate;

she knew that the flu could easily kill a tribal person with no immunity to foreign diseases.

As she prayed for guidance, Rachel remembered Dr. Ken Altig, a Wycliffe doctor she had worked with in Peru. Dr. Altig was on furlough in California, and Rachel was confident that he would be able to give her the best advice on how to treat Dayuma's illness. She tracked down Dr. Altig and, after talking to him by phone, followed his instructions to the letter. Within a few days Dayuma was showing signs of recovery. But her progress was slow, and Rachel spent many nights sitting beside Dayuma, coaxing her to drink a little water.

It was early November before Dayuma was strong enough to go outside again. Her first foray outdoors was for a very special reason—it was snowing. Dayuma was awestruck. In the rain forest she had never known anything colder than the mist that crawled up from the rivers and spread over the land in the early hours of the morning. But now she was surrounded by frozen water falling gently from the sky.

"I wish Sam were here," she told Rachel.

Rachel knew that Dayuma was homesick for her son. The two women discussed the matter, and Rachel promised to do her best to get Sam to join them in the United States. Of course, she knew it was a daunting task. Sam, like the Waorani and many other tribal people in the Amazon basin, had no official written record of his birth. This made getting a passport difficult, but Rachel did everything she could to handle the situation.

On November 18, 1957, stunning news awaited Rachel and Dayuma. It came by way of a phone call from Sam Saint in New York. Sam told Rachel that Betty Elliot wanted her to know that two Waorani women had walked out of the jungle. Although Rachel had a thousand questions, Sam did not have any more information than that, but he assured Rachel that Marj Saint, who was on furlough in California, would be calling her to fill her in on a few more details.

After waiting an hour or so, Rachel took matters into her hands and tracked down Marj. Even though it was predawn in California, Marj was happy to tell Rachel what she knew, although it was not much. According to Marj, Betty and her daughter Valerie were staying at a Quichua village when a Quichua woman brought two naked tribal women to her. Betty could tell straightaway that the women were Waoranis; they had the telltale round balsa wood plugs in their earlobes and spoke no Quichua at all. The woman who brought them to Betty said that a third person, a girl, had emerged from the jungle with them but had fled back into it when she was approached. Betty thought that one of the women was the older woman who had appeared in the photographs developed from Nate's recovered camera. This would make her Dayuma's aunt, Mintaka.

Rachel was delighted to think that more Waoranis had decided to trust the "outsiders," but Dayuma was distraught. "Tell your friends to take the visitors away to safety," she told Rachel. "My people will come and kill them."

This was a serious threat, and Rachel was sure that Dayuma was not being overly dramatic. She called up Marj again and asked her to relay Dayuma's warning to the radio operator at Shell Mera.

The one thing that did cheer Dayuma was the thought that the other woman might be her mother, and the runaway teenage girl her little sister Gimari.

Rachel could find no way, however, to persuade Dayuma to return to Ecuador immediately. Dayuma seemed too afraid to face her past, and she was not completely over the flu. Rachel decided it was wisest not to push Dayuma, but at the same time she was frustrated at the thought that she and Dayuma were the only two people who could communicate with the women, and they were thousands of miles away. Rachel did what she could. She suggested that Dayuma make a tape recording to be played to the two Waorani women back in Ecuador. Dayuma approved of the idea, and soon she was sitting tensely in front of a microphone.

"Long ago Moipa speared my father, and Umi, Aepi, and I fled from the jungle," Dayuma began. "My father was Tyaento. My mother was Akawo. I am Tyaento and Akawo's daughter Dayuma. Now I am living here with another who is like a relative. Here, far away, big-water other side I live. Later, returning I will come. Who are you two? I do not know."

Dayuma went on to urge the two women to trust Betty Elliot—the "tall woman with the white-haired baby"—and not to run back into the jungle. She asked them what rivers they lived on and whether her mother, sister, and brothers were still alive, ending with, "Long ago we did not live well, not loving God. Our old grandfather spoke and said that God created all things. All men and women He created. Yes, I now love that God. I now talk to that God. Now I live very well. Before I did not live well."

Rachel sent the tape off to Betty in Ecuador and waited anxiously for a reply. Before it arrived she heard from Marj once again. The call confirmed Dayuma's prediction. A Waorani raiding party had come out of the jungle and kidnapped the Quichua woman who had offered the two Waorani women refuge. They then speared the woman's husband to death with twenty-two spears. Following Dayuma's advice, the two Waorani women had been moved to Shandia before the attack took place to stay with Betty.

Strangely enough, Dayuma was relieved to hear the news of the killing. "Now that my people have taken a woman to replace the two that were lost, the killings will stop."

Finally a tape arrived at Sulphur Springs from Ecuador. Eagerly Rachel threaded it onto the tape machine and pushed the play button. Dayuma sat motionless in front of the machine waiting to hear the recorded voices. The tape, which had been recorded by Dr. Tidmarsh, was taped over a piano concerto that made the voices on the tape hard to understand at times. Still Dayuma sat transfixed and listened. Rachel listened also, but she found the tape hard to understand. She recognized a number of the Waorani words, but the voice on the tape spoke much faster than Dayuma and was much more high-pitched and nasally. At times Rachel wanted to stop the tape and rewind it to hear a portion of the speech again, but Dayuma would not allow it. She was eager to hear all that was on the tape recording.

Finally the tape drew to a close, and Dayuma relayed to Rachel all that was said on it. The woman who was speaking on the tape had identified herself as Maengamo, the wife of Dayuma's Uncle Gikita. And the woman who had fled with her was indeed Mintaka, Dayuma's aunt. But the girl who had fled back to the jungle turned out to be not a girl at all, but one of Maengamo's young brothers.

Maengamo had talked much about the continuing cycle of killing that went on inside the tribe and about the numerous atrocities carried out by Moipa. Maengamo also related how one day Moipa had been cornered and speared, but she did not say whether or not he was killed.

To Rachel's surprise, instead of exciting Dayuma, the tape seemed to send her into a downward spiral. Old hatred and fear began to surface in her conversation as she talked about her people. She was particularly upset to think that Moipa, her father's killer, might still be alive. As well, the fact that Maengamo had not indicated whether Dayuma's mother, Akawo, was alive or dead troubled her. Rachel did her best to encourage Dayuma, praying with and for her, but Dayuma continued to feel depressed.

When another tape arrived from Ecuador, Rachel nervously threaded it onto the tape player, hoping the contents of this tape would not upset Dayuma as much as the previous one had. Again Dayuma sat transfixed in front of the machine and listened. Once again, Maengamo was the main speaker, and as she had done on the previous tape recording, she recounted many of the killings that had gone on among the Waorani over the years. Then she relayed some information that caused Dayuma to yelp for joy. Moipa was indeed dead, speared by an angry mob several years before.

Dayuma's joy quickly subsided, however, when she learned that her big brother Wawae had been murdered. "He always brought me meat from the jungle, and I loved him very much," Dayuma told Rachel. As far as Dayuma knew, this left only her sisters Gimari and Oba and her brother Nampa alive.

The news of Wawae's death depressed Dayuma, and then her depression turned to anger. Rachel wanted her to go back into the jungle to share the gospel with her people, but Dayuma told Rachel that because of what had happened to her brother, she was no longer in a mood to agree to that request. "I will not return," she adamantly told Rachel.

Rachel was alarmed. She knew that bitterness had crept into Dayuma's heart. But without Dayuma it was difficult to imagine how she would ever make it safely into the Waorani tribe herself. So she thought and prayed about the matter. Finally, one day she said, "Dayuma, what if Jesus Christ had said, 'I will not go to those horrible people on earth. They are too wicked and sinful, and I cannot be bothered with them. I will stay in heaven with My Holy Father. It is a much better place than down on earth with all of those evil people.' What would have become of us if the Lord Jesus had said that?"

Chapter 11

Nimu

Rachel received no immediate response to her challenge, but she had not expected one. She knew that Dayuma would take several days to think through what she had said. Sure enough, several days later Dayuma finally said to Rachel, "When are we going back to my land? I want to go to my people and tell them about God."

Rachel was delighted and relieved. She had prayed hard that Dayuma would change her mind and let go of the bitterness she felt toward Moipa and others in her tribe. She also prayed about something else that would help to cheer Dayuma—her son Sam. Rachel had tried her best to get Sam to the United States, but her efforts had led nowhere. So when Larry Montgomery visited Sulphur Springs at the beginning of March 1958, Rachel wondered whether he might be part of the answer to her prayers. Larry had been instrumental in taking charge after Nate and the other four men were killed, and Rachel wondered whether he could help her to get Sam to the United States. She talked to him and explained the situation regarding Sam and asked if there was anything he could do to help. As he had done in Shell Mera, Larry started working immediately on a solution. Within two weeks he had cut through all the red tape, and Sam was soon reunited with his mother and Rachel at Sulphur Springs.

Dayuma was much more settled with her son by her side. And six-year-old Sam adjusted remarkably well to life in the United States. Within a few weeks of arriving he was able to make himself understood in simple English sentences.

Meanwhile, Rachel and Dayuma continued with their Waorani language work. Rachel had reached the stage where she was attempting to translate and write down in Waorani several stories from the New Testament. One of the stories she was working on was the story of the baptism of the Ethiopian eunuch in Acts 8. When she had translated the passage as accurately as she could, Rachel read it back to Dayuma. After sitting and thinking about the passage for several minutes, Dayuma repeated in Waorani the Ethiopian's request, "What does hinder me to be baptized?" and Philip's reply, "If you believe with all your heart, you may."

Rachel translated more stories from the New Testament into Waorani. Then two weeks after hearing the story of the baptism of the Ethiopian eunuch, Dayuma came to Rachel and asked, "What good man of God can enter me into the water?"

Rachel immediately thought of Dr. Edman, the president of Wheaton College in Illinois, who had long been interested in the Waorani. Dr. Edman had spent the previous Christmas in the Ecuadorian jungle and had written many articles and news reports about the Waorani. Rachel knew that Dr. Edman had a son living near Sulphur Springs, and she wrote to him and asked if he might be visiting his son anytime soon. If so, she asked, would he be available to come by and baptize Dayuma?

The reply she received from Dr. Edman was not what Rachel had expected. Dr. Edman was very excited about being asked to baptize Dayuma, but he saw the baptism as an opportunity to further the cause of reaching other Waorani with the gospel. To that end he proposed that Rachel and Dayuma fly to Wheaton, where Dayuma could be baptized in the Wheaton Evangelical Free Church. He pointed out that three of the five dead missionaries had many connections to Wheaton. Jim Elliot, Ed McCully, and Nate Saint had all attended Wheaton College, and the pastor of the church was Marj Saint's former pastor. Dr. Edman explained that, if Rachel agreed, he had arranged for a wealthy Christian businessman, R. G. LeTourneau, to fly Rachel, Dayuma, and Sam to Wheaton, Illinois, in his private airplane.

Once again Rachel was torn. She hated the idea of more publicity, more show. But she had to admit that Dr. Edman had a point. There was a sense of completion with the first Christian Waorani's being baptized in the place where three of the martyred men had trained. Rachel wrote back to Dr. Edman, agreeing to his proposal.

Soon the details of getting the three of them to Wheaton were being worked out. At the same time Rachel decided that it was long past the time for the three of them to return to the Oriente. She booked flights from Illinois to New York to visit her brother Sam and then flights from there back to Ecuador.

On April 14, 1958, Rachel, Dayuma, and Sam found themselves surrounded by friends of the cause of reaching the Waorani with the gospel. Rachel's parents were among those who witnessed the baptism, as was Ed McCully's mother. Jim Elliot's parents had come all the way from California for the occasion. Wheaton College had also dispatched press releases announcing the baptism, and since Rachel and Dayuma were still in the public eye following their appearance on *This Is Your Life,* newspapers from across the country picked up on the event and relayed it to millions of people. Once again, Rachel and Dayuma found themselves the center of attention, something Rachel always did her best to avoid.

After the baptism, Rachel, Dayuma, and Sam flew from Chicago to New York City, where they were guests of Sam Saint and photographer Cornell Capa. Cornell told Rachel that the publishing company of Harper and Row was eager to publish Rachel's biography, but Rachel refused to entertain the idea. The last thing she wanted was more publicity.

Following their stopover in New York at the end of May 1958, Rachel, Dayuma, and Sam boarded another airplane and flew south. As they got closer to Ecuador, Rachel watched Dayuma's excitement about going home slowly turn to nervousness as she contemplated meeting her relatives. Finally she turned to Rachel and said, "I will call you Nimu. It means star, and it was the name of my little sister who was hacked to death by Moipa."

Rachel nodded, unsure of what the point was of being given the new name.

Dayuma went on. "That will make you my sister, and being my sister, you are also their relative. They will not spear their relative."

Rachel smiled reassuringly. She appreciated how much Dayuma cared for her safety. "Nimu is a lovely name," she replied.

"And to our relatives, you must never ask about the men who killed your brother," Dayuma added. "Hearing this, my people will think you want revenge. And then they will have to kill you first."

Again Rachel nodded. All she could do was trust that God would lead her into the Waorani tribe at the right time, as the way was filled with pitfalls, all of which appeared to end with her death at the end of a spear.

Once the three of them arrived back in Ecuador, rather than going back to Hacienda San Carlos,

Rachel arranged for them to go to Limoncocha, where Wycliffe's new Dawson Trotman Memorial Base, the mission's center of operations for Ecuador, was located. Limoncocha was situated thirty miles north of the Rio Napo, on the edge of Waorani territory.

Rachel, Dayuma, and Sam settled in to their new home and awaited the arrival of Mintaka and Maengamo, along with Betty and Valerie Elliot, from Shandia. As they waited, Rachel observed Dayuma becoming more moody with each passing day.

"What if coming, they bring bad news?" Dayuma finally asked.

Rachel had no way of reassuring Dayuma except to urge her to pray for peace.

Finally, late one morning the radio crackled to life to deliver the message that the plane carrying Mintaka, Maengamo, Betty, and Valerie was on its way from Shandia. Dayuma raced to the airstrip, where she waited impatiently, her eyes constantly in motion scanning the horizon for any sign of the plane. After several minutes Rachel caught up to her at the side of the airstrip. They heard the aircraft before they saw it. As its engine droned across the jungle, Rachel laid her hand on Dayuma's shoulder to both calm and encourage her.

Soon the plane was bouncing down the runway toward them. As it taxied to a halt in front of them, Rachel could see the excited dark faces of the two Waorani women pressed against the window. As soon as the engine stopped, the door of the aircraft swung open, and Mintaka and Maengamo jumped out and bounded over to Dayuma.

Mintaka and Maengamo both talked over each other as they greeted Dayuma. They stood in the shadow of the wing, talking furiously for several minutes before Rachel suggested that they move to the hut at the edge of the jungle where the women were going to stay.

Mintaka, Maengamo, and Dayuma sat in the shade of a kapok tree all afternoon talking. Rachel watched from a distance, amazed at how furious and animated their conversation was. As dusk approached, the three women lit a fire and roasted some yucca root to eat.

A thick blanket of darkness settled over the Oriente, and still the women talked on. Finally, after midnight their conversation trailed off, and Dayuma crawled into her hammock in the hut she shared with Rachel.

"You have talked a long time," Rachel commented. "What have you learned from Mintaka and Maengamo about your tribe?"

"I have learned many sad things. There has been so much killing among my people. When one person is killed, that person's death must be retaliated against. And so the killing never seems to stop," Dayuma replied with a sigh. "I am sad, too, because my brother Nampa is dead. But a spear did not kill him. One day in the jungle an anaconda attacked him. The great snake crushed him badly. He was able to kill it and escape its grasp, but he was badly bruised and injured. For one month he lingered in much agony, and then he died. I am sad because he did not know God like I do."

Rachel reached out and laid her hand on Dayuma's arm to comfort her.

"But there is good news, too, Rachel, and it makes me happy," Dayuma added.

"And what is the good news?" Rachel asked.

"My mother, Akawo, is not dead after all; she is alive! And for the twelve years I have been gone she has been searching for me. My people told her, 'Give up this belief. Dayuma is dead. She went to the outside, and the cowadi have surely eaten her. That is what they do. They eat those who come to them from the jungle.' But Akawo would not believe them. She believed that I was alive. She sent my brother Wawae to look for me, but he could not find me. Then she wanted to come to the outside to find me, but my uncle would not let her go. 'The cowadi will eat you. You must not go,' he said. But now Akawo has sent Mintaka and Maengamo to the outside to find me. And they have."

Tears gathered in the corners of Rachel's eyes as she listened to Dayuma's words. She knew how tortured Dayuma had been over the years, worrying whether her mother was still alive. And now Dayuma knew that she was.

By the time Rachel crawled out of her hammock the following morning, Dayuma was already up and sitting beside the fire with Mintaka and Maengamo, engaged again in animated conversation.

Rachel moved closer to hear what they were talking about, and what she heard surprised and delighted her. Dayuma was telling Mintaka and Maengamo about God.

"The God our grandfather used to tell us about—I know Him now!" Dayuma said. Then she proceeded to relate to them many of the Bible stories Rachel had told her.

For many days Dayuma, Mintaka, and Maengamo talked together. By late August the three of them were making plans to return to the jungle, since Mintaka and Maengamo had promised Akawo that they would return when the kapok was ripe.

Rachel was delighted by this turn of events, and she asked about the possibility of their taking her and Betty Elliot, who had made great progress in learning the Waorani language, with them. But Dayuma refused to let them go along. "It is too dangerous. I myself go not knowing what will become of me. Wait. We will return for you," she told Rachel.

Dayuma even asked Rachel if she could leave Sam with her, fearing that it would be too dangerous for him to go with her.

On September 2, 1958, Dayuma, Mintaka, and Maengamo set out for Waorani territory. After saying a prayer for their safety and success on the journey, Rachel, with Sam at her side, and Betty and her daughter Valerie stood and watched the three Waorani women walk off into the jungle. Soon the women were no longer visible as the dense foliage swallowed them up like some great monster. They had left on a full moon, and Dayuma promised that she would return on the next full moon. "I hope and pray that they are successful in their mission and that they will return to us soon," Rachel muttered to herself and to Betty.

Following the women's departure, Betty and Valerie returned to Shandia, and Rachel and Sam went to Lago Agria to stay with some Wycliffe friends.

Several days after Dayuma, Mintaka, and Maengamo had set out, an MAF plane with Betty aboard flew over Waorani territory to see whether they could spot the three women on the ground.

"I saw no sign of them on the ground," Betty reported to Rachel by radio.

"We'll just have to keep praying and trusting God," Rachel replied.

"I will take another flight over their territory in a week and see if I can spot them then," Betty said.

Rachel spent an anxious week continuing with her Waorani translation of various Bible stories and entertaining Sam. Finally, late one afternoon the radio crackled to life, and Rachel raced over to hear what Betty had to report. Betty had made another pass over Waorani territory and unfortunately still had not spotted Dayuma, Mintaka, or Maengamo, or any other Waoranis for that matter.

After she had finished talking to Betty on the radio, Rachel sat outside under a palm tree as the setting sun turned the clouds that hovered above the Oriente into puffs of gold. But she hardly even noticed the sunset. With her thoughts far away in the jungle in Waorani territory, she was wondering what might have happened to Dayuma. Was her friend alive, or had she been speared to death like so many other members of her tribe? Rachel wished she knew what had happened to Dayuma, but she did not, and she would just have to wait and pray and hope.

Chapter 12

Watching the Vision Come True

It was midmorning September 25, 1958, when the radio at Lago Agria again crackled to life. Rachel immediately ran to it just in time to hear Betty calling from Arajuno, saying, "Come in, Rachel. Over."

"I'm here, Betty. Go ahead. Over," Rachel said into the radio mouthpiece.

"Wonderful news," Betty exclaimed. "Dayuma has come out of the jungle with Mintaka and Maengamo, another woman, and a handful of girls and boys. They are inviting you and me and Valerie to come and live with them. Over."

Rachel sat down abruptly. "Thank God they're safe," she replied. "Is Dayuma's mother with her? Over."

"I don't think so," Betty replied. "But it's all a bit of a jumble at the moment, and Dayuma wants to talk to you. When can you come? Over."

"I'll start packing right now! Over," Rachel laughed, jubilant that things appeared to be working out and astounded that ten Waoranis had trusted Dayuma enough to risk exposing themselves to foreigners.

As soon as the radio conversation was over, Rachel called Sam and told him the good news, and then they started packing.

Soon after lunch a Wycliffe airplane picked up Rachel and Sam and flew them to Arajuno, where they had a joyous reunion with Dayuma. They all talked long into the night. Rachel was particularly relieved to learn that Dayuma had convinced her Uncle Gikita to return the Quichua widow who had been taken captive. The group had escorted the woman out of the jungle and taken her to her home village on their way to Arajuno.

On October 3, Rachel wrote to her parents:

> You have probably heard by now that Dayuma, along with Mintaka and Maengamo, plus one of Naenkiwi's wives and baby, and three girls and two boys arrived at Arajuno last Thursday.... Dayuma was in the lead, singing, 'Jesus loves me, this I know'—*in English!* By the time I got here, she was pretty keyed up, and it has taken me a while to get the picture in focus. She brought

> an invitation for Betty and me to return with them and has given orders about building a house for us.... She just told me tonight about her trip.

Rachel put her pen down and thought. It was almost impossible to put into words all of the things Dayuma had recounted about the trip back to her people. Dayuma had told Rachel that it had been a long and difficult walk for her, mainly because she was no longer used to hacking her way through thick jungle, clambering over logs, and shimmying down muddy slopes. By the time she reached the bank of the Tiwaeno River, Dayuma was exhausted. Maengamo offered to go and find Dayuma's mother and bring her to the riverbank. For two tense days Dayuma and Mintaka waited for Maengamo to return. And then, just as it was getting dark on the second day, Dayuma heard the unmistakable yodel of her mother. Akawo and Dayuma were both overcome with emotion as they embraced each other. Then with a nervous giggle, Akawo poked at Dayuma's clothes and commented on how tall she had grown.

After it got dark, Dayuma explained, two more members of her extended family arrived. And over the next several days, more than fifty adults and children from Dayuma's extended family gathered at the makeshift camp on the bank of the Tiwaeno River. Everyone marveled that Dayuma had been treated well by the outsiders and had all sorts of questions for her. Why hadn't the cowadi killed her and eaten her? What else did they eat? How were wood-bees (airplanes) made? And was it true that Dayuma had been across a great water wider than the Curaray River?

Dayuma spent hours every night describing her experiences as best she could to her relatives, though the Waorani language did not have names for many of the things she talked about. No one had ever seen a car or any other mechanical vehicle, other than an airplane overhead, or even imagined that such things existed. Dayuma told how many foreigners lived in very big groups, so big that they did not even know each other's names, and that they did not walk on trails. Instead they sat down inside "wood-bees that go on the ground" and these wood-bees went very fast in large groups all going the same way. She also told them that foreigners loved to "carve on wood" (write on paper) and that Rachel spent many hours each day doing just that. She explained that Rachel was doing this because she wanted to carve God's words on wood so that the Waorani could see them anytime they wanted.

This idea of God's wanting to give them carvings amazed Dayuma's family, and they plied Dayuma with more questions. Dayuma answered their questions as best she could and then countered with a question of her own. Would her family welcome Rachel and Betty if she brought them into the jungle to meet them? After Dayuma assured everyone that Rachel and Betty truly were "good foreigners," the family agreed that the two women would be safe if Dayuma went and brought them back with her.

It took Rachel and Betty ten days to gather everything they would need to enter and live in the jungle. While they planned to eat the jungle diet of manioc, monkey meat, bananas, and various roots, they did pack tea and coffee to take with them. Betty also packed a large supply of powdered milk for Valerie to drink, as well as several notebooks, a camera, and rolls of film. The biggest items Rachel packed to take with her were a portable typewriter and a two-way radio, which would be their only way of communicating with the outside world. In addition, arrangements were made for Sam to attend boarding school in Quito, where the Bible Missionary Society had agreed to pay his tuition.

On Monday, October 6, 1958, a band of eighteen people set out from Arajuno, bound for Waorani territory. The group consisted of Rachel, Betty and Valerie, Dayuma, Mintaka and Maengamo and the seven other Waoranis who had come out of the jungle with them, and five Quichua men who served as porters. One of the Quichua men was assigned to carry three-year-old Valerie in a sling on his back.

The Waoranis and Quichuas were adept at moving speedily through the jungle and over rough terrain, far more adept than Rachel and Betty. For much of the journey into Waorani territory, the two missionary women rode in a dugout canoe while the Waoranis made their way along the river's edge. But even as swiftly as the current swept along the canoe, the Waoranis seemed to have no trouble keeping up with it.

The vegetation along the edge of the river was thick, lush, and tangled, and at times the Waoranis and Quichuas had to stop and hack a trail ahead with their machetes. Beyond the vegetation at the river's edge, tall trees reached toward the sky, creating a canopy above that was so thick it blocked the sun, leaving the jungle floor in almost perpetual darkness. The jungle was untouched, with no roads or settlements. Because of the Waoranis' fearsome reputation, few outsiders had ever passed through the area. Rachel marveled at the abundance of wildlife that filled the jungle. Monkeys and birds danced in the treetops, howling, and chirping at each other, and larger animals, such as tapirs and jaguars, came to drink at the water's edge. Everywhere butterflies fluttered above the river, their brightly decorated bodies gleaming in the hot, tropical sun.

After two days of grueling travel, the group reached the Tiwaeno River, a tributary of the Curaray, and began working their way up the smaller river. Finally they came to a place where the canoe could go no farther, and Rachel and Betty had to leave it behind on the sandy bank of the river and head overland on foot. They had to climb up and over a steep ridge, beyond which Dayuma told them her family's settlement lay. It was quite a climb up the narrow, slippery track that led to the top of the ridge, and Rachel was very relieved when they reached the summit. However, descending the other side of the ridge was even more difficult than climbing it. The track was steeper, and huge tree roots stretched across it. While the Waoranis seemed to glide effortlessly over the roots, Rachel and Betty were left to clamber clumsily over them, being careful not to reach up and grasp the vines that hung from the tree above them when they lost their balance. The vines were home to many dangerous and well-camouflaged snakes.

Eventually the group came to a place where Dayuma stopped and pointed out the clearing below, dotted with thatched huts. That was where Dayuma's relatives were waiting for them to arrive. As they got closer to the clearing, a naked man and two women emerged from one of the huts and stood waiting. Rachel felt her heart skip a beat as she looked at these three Waoranis anxiously awaiting her arrival. The scene so resembled the vision she had had while standing on the deck of the *Aquitania* twenty-seven years before. In her vision Rachel had seen a group of native people in the jungle beckoning her to come to them, and now here she was, watching the vision come true. It was almost too much to take in.

Suddenly Dayuma let out a whoop of delight. "This is Nimu," she said, grabbing Rachel by the hand and pulling her toward the three naked Waoranis.

The trio turned out to be Dayuma's Uncle Kimo, his wife, Dawa, and Dayuma's younger sister Gimari.

"Where are Akawo and the others?" Dayuma inquired. Rachel could hear a note of panic in her voice. How sad it would be to find that some violent attack had wiped them all out just when they were opening up to the outside world.

"They went downriver to find food," Kimo explained. "They will be back tomorrow or the next day. I remained here to welcome the foreigners we hoped would come."

Before leaving Arajuno, Dayuma had confided in Rachel that the men who had killed Nate and the other four missionaries had been from her extended family and that Kimo was one of those men. Now Rachel found herself looking into the eyes of the man who may well have speared her brother to death. But strangely, as she stared at Kimo, Rachel felt not anger but compassion toward him. From her perspective Kimo had acted out of ignorance. He was trapped in a way of life that found glory in senseless killing. But with God's help, Rachel intended to break that cycle of murder and hatred through the life-changing power of the gospel.

When night fell, everyone gathered around a fire, and the porters began to sing Quichua hymns. Dayuma's relatives sat transfixed, staring at the sight of five men singing together in unison. Rachel realized that they had never heard a language other than Waorani, nor had they ever heard someone singing a melody.

When the hymn singing ended, the Quichuas announced that they were going to pray. The man who had carried Valerie stood up and began, "Thank You for bringing us safely to these new friends. Show us how to live together like brothers."

As the group talked on into the night, Dayuma informed Rachel that while she was gone, one of the women of the tribe, Mima, had died from a cold. Dayuma told Rachel that no one at the Waorani settlement had ever had a cold before. Rachel realized that Dayuma and the other women must have brought the virus to the tribe. This was something that Rachel had feared, and she hoped that the Waoranis' contact with the outside world would not end in many deaths because they had so little immunity to outside diseases.

As the embers of the fire died away, everyone prepared to sleep. Since so many members of the tribe were still downriver, there was plenty of sleeping space for everyone. Rachel and Dayuma hung their hammocks in the hut with Dayuma's Uncle Kimo, Dawa, Gimari, and several others. Betty moved into another hut with Valerie, and the five Quichua men all found hammocks for themselves in other empty huts and settled in for the night.

The night was still as Rachel lay down in her hammock. Over the soft breathing of the dozen or so other people in the hut, Rachel could hear crickets chirping and monkeys howling in the distance. As she lay there, going over in her mind the amazing events of the day, she counted up how long it had been since Nate and the other four men had been killed. She soon realized that it had been thirty-three months to the day. And how much had happened in those thirty-three months!

Dayuma had become a Christian and been baptized in Wheaton, Illinois. And if that were not enough, Dayuma had also met Billy Graham and spoken to over 16,000 people at one of his crusades in Madison Square Garden in New York. And now, perhaps more amazing than anything, Rachel was lying in a hammock in a hut full of Waoranis who had invited her to come and live among them. It was almost too much to take in. Rachel drifted off to sleep, not knowing what amazing things the following day would bring.

Chapter 13

Among the Waorani

At dawn the following day, Rachel listened as Kimo climbed out of his hammock and said a few words to Dawa, his wife, before disappearing into the jungle.

"Where is he going?" Rachel asked.

"Going, he will return with the others," Dawa replied.

Rachel lay in her hammock for a few more minutes until the golden glow of the morning sun filtered through the towering kapok and ironwood trees. She could hear the younger girls outside giggling and splashing as they filled clay pots with water. Then came the low chanting of Gimari as she poked the fire back to life and threw some corncobs onto it. Rachel could hear in the adjacent hut

Valerie's high-pitched voice chattering away to her mother. "Mommy, may I play in the water today?" To Rachel the early-morning scene seemed so normal and yet so strange at the same time.

The Quichua porters had decided to leave that afternoon, and before they left, they busied themselves making a narrow bamboo bed for Rachel. Several Waorani boys trotted upriver to spear fish, and the women crossed the river to dig yucca from an old, abandoned garden clearing.

Rachel looked for every opportunity to practice her language skills, though she found that the other members of the tribe spoke much faster than Dayuma did. As she sat on a balsa log, rebraiding her long hair, Gimari sat down beside her.

"Dayuma lived at my house," Rachel told her. "She is like my little sister. Now we are happy to be here."

Gimari did not reply.

That afternoon, as the Quichua porters prepared to leave the village and head back to the "outside" world, Rachel sat down to write a letter to her parents. Seated on a log with a pad balanced on her knees, she began,

> The welcome could not have been more friendly. You'd think these bronze girls were debutantes entertaining and that this happened every day. They are really charmers. Kimo's wife has no children yet. Gimari has a darling fat baby, Bai, who is another of Naenkiwi's children.

Rachel stopped for a moment and looked around, trying to find the words to describe how she felt about finally getting to the tribe.

> It seems the most natural thing in the world to me to be here, a thing I felt the Lord was leading me to over five years ago. Do pray that this situation will be workable and will accomplish the Lord's purposes....
>
> Kimo's wife, Dawa, is from the downriver group. Although the natural situation would never take her back to them, I pray that she may be one of the contacts that will lead them to Him too. It is a larger group than this one, and they speak the same language.

When the letter was finished and addressed, the Quichua porters gathered to pray and then disappeared down the trail into the jungle. Rachel, Betty, and Valerie watched them leave. Rachel was sure that Betty was thinking the same thing she was: the radio was now their only link to the outside. For the first time, they were alone among the Waorani without any male protection. Rachel did not let herself dwell on the thought, though she knew that a missionary couple had gone to the Nhambiquara Indians in Brazil some years before and had lived peacefully with them for two years before the Indians turned on them and hacked the husband and baby to death.

To Rachel, everything here looked happy and welcoming on the outside, but she had no way of knowing what was going on inside the heads of the Waoranis who surrounded her and Betty and Valerie. As she returned to sit near the fire—and enjoy the smoky protection it offered against mosquitoes—Rachel prayed that whatever happened to her personally, the gospel would penetrate the hearts of Dayuma's tribal family.

Just before sunset, shouts were heard coming from farther up the Tiwaeno River.

"They are coming!" Dayuma exclaimed as she jumped up. "Come on, Nimu. Let's meet them."

The entire group ran down to the riverbank and peered into the tangled jungle, looking for the first signs of Kimo and whoever was with him. Soon they heard a rustling among the undergrowth, and then suddenly a group of Waoranis emerged onto the narrow beach on the other side of the river. Among them was Akawo, who, when she saw Dayuma, waded across the river as fast as she could. Rachel watched as Akawo, her body shaking with emotion, greeted her daughter.

Akawo was eager to meet Rachel as well, and soon Dayuma was introducing them.

"You are Nimu," Akawo said. "You came down from the sky. You must call me Mother."

Rachel smiled and took a long look at her new "mother." She was surprised that Akawo was much older than she had imagined. Akawo's face was weathered and wrinkled, but a happy, open smile was etched into the corners of her mouth. And although Akawo arrived wearing the cotton dress, albeit dirty and crumpled by now, that Dayuma had brought her on the first visit, she stripped it off soon after meeting Rachel, leaving her completely naked except for a few small pieces of native jewelry.

The following day Dayuma's younger sister Oba, her husband, Dyuwi, and baby daughter Adyibae joined the group. Dayuma's Uncle Gikita, his two young sons, Komi and Koni, and her half brother Minkayi and his family followed them. Within a week about fifty members of Dayuma's extended family had settled in and around the clearing in the jungle beside the Tiwaeno River.

Life soon fell into a pattern at the new village. Everyone had a job to do and busied himself doing it. For the men, much of their time was taken up hunting meat in the jungle. Rachel soon learned that the more men there were, the better everyone ate. Mostly the men used poisoned darts fired from a blowpipe to catch their prey, which consisted primarily of monkeys and wild hogs. And everyone tried his or her hand at spearing fish in the river. The children also caught fish with their hands in the streams that fed into the river, while the women cultivated yucca and bananas and gathered firewood. Rachel was amazed at the bounty the jungle provided to eat. Often a group would go off into the jungle in search of bees' nests and would bring back gourd bowls filled with honey.

One day Kimo came running into the clearing and announced that he had killed a prized amunga monkey with his blowpipe. But alas, the creature had fallen into the hollow center of a large tree, and

Kimo needed help to retrieve it. Soon a large group of people had formed to help Kimo, and Dayuma invited Rachel to go along. Happily and loudly the group followed Kimo through the jungle to the tree in question. When they got there, Kimo and several of the boys in the group surveyed the situation, and then they got to work. First they chopped down several smaller trees to clear a place for the large tree to fall. Then they began hacking at the trunk of the large tree with their machetes. Soon the tree came crashing to the ground, much to the delight of everybody. Kimo ran over to it and retrieved the carcass of the monkey he had killed. Then he discovered an added bonus. Deep down in the hollow trunk two porcupines were hiding. Since they were too far down for anyone to reach them, a fire was lit to try to smoke them out.

As the attempt was made, the Waoranis chattered and giggled among themselves. Rachel marveled at how happy and content they seemed to be and how they all worked together to retrieve the dead monkey and to try to smoke out the porcupines. It was hard for her to imagine at that moment that this was a tribe of people who could ruthlessly turn on each other with their spears.

When, despite the smoke, the porcupines refused to budge from the hollow tree trunk, it was decided to leave them there and head back to the village. After all, the people had an amunga monkey, and they would eat well.

Most of the things the Waoranis ate, Rachel could eat. But she drew the line at eating monkey heads.

She could eat the monkeys' roasted, hairy legs, but the heads reminded her of the shrunken heads the Shapra Indians produced from the severed heads of their enemies. Rachel soon learned that the Waoranis were not insulted by her not eating the monkey heads. To them monkey heads were a delicacy, and the fewer people who ate them, the more there was for the others to eat. So they never pressed her to eat the heads.

Each day seemed to pass pretty much as the day before, unless a tapir, deer, or wild hog was speared. Then a feast was in order.

For Rachel and Betty the days were filled with language study and the daily work of staying alive and clean in the jungle. Unlike the Waoranis, the two women had clothes to wash and hang out to dry on nearby bushes, and letters to write in the hope that they would soon find a way to get them to a post office.

Rachel also took on the task of drawing a family tree for the tribe. The tribe was more tangled than even she could have imagined. The Waoranis used the same words for father and uncle and for mother and aunt. This made things extremely difficult, as did the fact that men could be married to more than one woman. Many facts emerged as Rachel asked questions about kinship and was faced with the brutality of the revenge system. Rachel noted that Dayuma's mother, Akawo, had seen her father, a brother, two sisters, and a husband, son, daughter, and son-in-law speared to death, as well as many other more distant relatives.

In the process of this research, Rachel also learned the identities of all the men who speared Nate and the other four men to death: Dayuma's uncles Gikita and Kimo, Nimonga, Dyuwi, and Minkayi. Rachel also learned the events that had led up to the killing. The harrowing story was one of treachery and ignorance.

Naenkiwi and Gimari, whom the five missionaries on Palm Beach had referred to as George and Delilah, had wanted to marry, but Akawo did not like Naenkiwi and would not give them permission to marry. This had upset Gimari, who told her mother that if she did not change her mind about the wedding, she would run away to the cowadi who had dropped gifts to them from the wood-bee in the sky and were now camped on the Curaray. But Akawo just laughed at her daughter, and in a rage Gimari set off through the jungle. Naenkiwi soon set out after her. However, in Waorani culture it is a bad thing for an unmarried man and woman to be alone together, so Mintaka—Dayuma and Gimari's aunt—followed them. The three of them arrived at Palm Beach together, where they met the cowadi, who turned out to be a strange group of people but not dangerous. Repeatedly Gimari asked the cowadi to take her in the wood-bee to visit her sister Dayuma, but the cowadi did not understand. And then late in the afternoon, the wood-bee had flown away without Gimari. Again, Gimari had stormed off in a rage, and Naenkiwi had followed her. But Mintaka decided to stay with the cowadi for the night. In the morning, she reasoned, perhaps the cowadi would take her in the wood-bee to see her niece Dayuma. But when she awoke in the morning, the wood-bee was not at the beach, so she left too.

Back at the village the following morning, Naenkiwi made up lies about the cowadi to cover the fact that he had been alone with Gimari throughout the night. He told those at the village that the cowadi had attacked the three of them and wanted to kill and eat them. He and Gimari had run in the same direction, but Mintaka had run in another direction. The three of them had become separated, and Naenkiwi and Gimari had been forced to spend the night together. But that point was not important, Naenkiwi had pointed out. What was important was that a group of dangerous cowadi had invaded their territory, intent on harming them, just as all the other cowadi had done in the past, and they must do something about it.

The Waorani had hoped that the cowadi in the yellow wood-bee would be friendly. After all, they had dropped many gifts to them. But now they knew that that was not true; Naenkiwi had told them so.

"This is the work of a clever enemy," Gikita had told everyone. "Only a clever enemy would pretend to be friendly and then attack. With their wood-bee and gifts, these cowadi are extra clever!"

Gikita went on to recall all the awful things other cowadi had done to them throughout the years. His stories whipped the young men of the village into a frenzy of hate, and the men began to sharpen new spears with which to spear the cowadi on the banks of the Curaray River.

When Mintaka eventually arrived back at the village, she told everyone that Naenkiwi had lied, that these were peaceful cowadi. But it was too late. In their frenzied state, the men set out for the Curaray.

The Waorani men found Nate and the other four missionaries resting on the beach. They used three women who had gone with them as decoys to wade across the river and engage the cowadis' attention while the men crept around behind the missionaries and speared them. Within minutes all five cowadi had been speared to death. The enemy that had invaded the Waoranis' territory was beaten, and the group were soon headed back to the village to celebrate.

Rachel also learned that Naenkiwi, whose lies had led to the killings on Palm Beach, had himself been speared and died about a year after the attack on the five men.

As she delved deeper into the family tree of the group, Rachel was confronted with how devastating the constant killing had been on the family. When she left her people twelve years before, Dayuma estimated that there had been about two hundred members in her extended family. Now, Rachel discovered, approximately forty of Dayuma's relatives were still alive. And most of the 160 who were dead had been killed by spears.

If that were not enough, Rachel soon came face-to-face with the horror of how easily one Waorani would spear another to death. When one of the small boys in the village died, Rachel discovered his father, Tidonca, sharpening a spear made from a chonta palm. When she asked Tidonca what he was doing, he replied, "My son has died. Why should my worthless daughter live?"

Realizing that Tidonca was planning to kill his daughter and bury her with the body of his son—a common practice among the Waorani—Rachel ran to Tidonca, snatched the spear from him, and fled into the jungle. When Rachel finally dared to return to her hut with the spear several hours later, she found Kimo there, standing guard to protect her from Tidonca's anger.

Rachel hoped and prayed that her actions would not lead to the death of Kimo. Fortunately they did not. With no spear, Tidonca decided not to kill his daughter, and after he had buried his son, his anger at Rachel subsided.

The following day Rachel returned Tidonca's spear. It was a gesture of trust. Tidonca could easily have turned around and used it against Rachel. But he seemed to grasp the nature of the gesture. He accepted the spear, and he and Rachel became good friends.

As time went on, Rachel became more burdened by the challenges she faced translating the Scriptures into Waorani. The job became more daunting with each passing day. The tribe had no concept of buying, selling, or trading. If there was food left over, it was shared with others. If not, it was all eaten by the family of the person who hunted for it or gathered it. The people also had no job designations, such as fisherman, teacher, farmer, tax collector, tentmaker, or artisan. To introduce such words to them, Rachel had to explain a whole different world.

Rachel labored over decisions about what to label things. She tried to keep words as simple as she could, but it was impossible. Since the tribe had no word for paper or bread, they used the same word, *wasp's nest,* since a wasp's nest looks a little like both. Paper money thus became "wasp's nest which is given-taken." Then there was the matter of what was "given-taken" in Bible stories. And apart from Dayuma, no one had ever seen a donkey, sheep, or horse, and trying to explain the difference between these animals was especially frustrating for Rachel. At times she wondered whether she would ever produce a New Testament translation.

Rachel and Betty relied heavily on Dayuma's help. In a sense Dayuma became the central missionary to her tribe. She began to explain to the group things about the outside world. She taught them to count off the days in units of seven, as they did in the outside world. Then at dawn on the first day, she held a church service in Kimo and Dawa's hut. People would lounge in their hammocks or sit on the floor or on a log outside as Dayuma told them Bible stories and about "God's Carving" (the Bible). Dayuma also taught the people to sing short, one-line hymns, or rather chant them in a nasally, minor key, the Waorani version of singing. She also led the group in long prayers. This idea took the members of the group a long time to get used to since they had no concept of addressing God directly. Dayuma would tell everyone while she prayed to close his or her eyes as though going to sleep. If people began to talk during the prayer, Dayuma would interrupt herself and in no uncertain terms tell those who were talking to be quiet.

Rachel watched the faces of the Waorani as Dayuma spoke to them about God. At first the people seemed to betray no emotion or interest in what was being said. But as the weeks rolled by, Rachel began to see some of the people become more interested and engaged. Among those who seemed to be listening more thoughtfully to what Dayuma said were Gikita and Kimo and Dawa.

As Rachel continued her translation work, conceptual breakthroughs in her understanding of how the Waorani thought often occurred in the most unlikely ways. One day Akawo asked Rachel, "Does God stay in his hammock away up there in the sky?"

Rachel thought for a minute and asked herself: Why not think of there being hammocks in the house God is thatching for them up there? It was as good as any interpretation she could come up with, and it was an interpretation she knew the Waoranis would be able to get their thoughts around.

Rachel and Betty had been in the jungle for two and a half months when they decided they needed a break from the harsh realities of jungle living, and from each other. Rachel thought Betty was the most stubborn person she had ever met, and Betty told Rachel she felt the same about her. They often clashed over the best way to go about the translation work, and by December 1958 they were both exhausted. Rachel and Dayuma headed to Limoncocha while Betty and Valerie went to stay with Marilou McCully at a guest house in Quito.

Rachel and Dayuma arrived back at the village first, and Betty returned in March 1959 with a letter for Rachel from Cameron Townsend. In the letter, Uncle Cam told Rachel that he had found someone to write the story of Dayuma's life. The writer was Emily Wallis, a fellow Wycliffe worker. Emily had just completed writing the book *Two Thousand Tongues to Go,* which told the story of Wycliffe Bible Translators since its founding. Rachel had mixed feelings about Uncle Cam's book idea. Although she felt that Dayuma's life story was worth writing about, Rachel was wary of what more exposure to the outside might do to the fragile Waorani tribe.

Chapter 14

Spiritual Changes

Rachel glanced at the calendar hanging on the woven bamboo wall. It was April 17, 1960, Easter Sunday. The calendar and the radio messages she received from the outside world were the only way Rachel could tell one day from another. Dayuma was still trying to get her people to count off the days in increments of seven so that they could have Sunday once a week, but it was an uphill battle. People would forget to count a day and then start from the beginning again, so that some "weeks" were ten or twelve days long.

Clapping and chanting started outside as Rachel wound her long hair into a bun, reached for her Bible, and walked across the clearing to where Dayuma had gathered a crowd. The people were singing one of the songs Dayuma had made up for them. When the singing had finished, Dayuma started talking to the people about God's Carvings, as she often did. In ten minutes she had covered the birth, life, death, and resurrection of Jesus Christ. Then she gave a warning: "All of you, not believing, will be thrown out of heaven, just as you throw worms out of your corn. Do you understand? Not believing, the devil will snatch you."

Dayuma then turned and looked each person in the eye. "Who will say, 'Yes, I love God. Yes, I believe. Yes, I want to live well and take God's trail to heaven?'" she asked.

Several green parrots alighted on a nearby kapok tree as Dayuma went on. "Will you, Dawa?"

"Yes," Dawa answered, her voice strong and certain.

"And Gimari? Will you also take God's trail?"

"Yes, I will love God too," Gimari replied.

Dayuma continued around the group in the same manner, but no one else wanted to join Dawa and Gimari.

Still, Rachel was delighted. Just eighteen months had passed since she come to live with the tribe, and now two people had decided to become Christians. Later that night Rachel walked down to the river alone and wept for joy. All of the heartache had been worth it to hear Dawa and Gimari speak up in the church meeting.

Rachel and Dayuma started teaching the two new converts from the Bible, and Dayuma prayed with them every day. The converts' progress was slow but steady, and although no other Waorani joined them in their new faith, all of Dayuma's family became more relaxed around Rachel. Their suspicions of her motives for coming to the tribe—especially revenge for the killing of her brother—began to slip away.

Rachel and Dayuma made another trip to Limoncocha in January, and when they returned, Kimo rushed to meet them on the trail. He was beaming from ear to ear.

"We counted the days, and on God's day we spoke God's Carvings to one another," he said.

Rachel squeezed Kimo's hand—and wondered whether he would be the next Christian convert in the group.

That Sunday Dayuma spoke to the group about forgiveness. "Look at that monkey out there," she said, pointing to a pet howler monkey one of the children had tied to a tree with a vine. "It is tied with a vine, just the same way we are tied to our sins until God cuts the vine and sets us free. See the water in the little river? When we are believing in Jesus, our sins are buried in water deeper than that."

Then she told the story of meeting Chief Tariri in the United States and finding out that he had been a headhunter before he became a believer. "Now he teaches his people about God," Dayuma told the group.

Later that morning Rachel made her scheduled radio transmission to Limoncocha to update the mission leaders there on her situation. When the transmission was finished, she turned the large knob on the radio and quickly scanned the dial for any other transmissions, though she seldom picked up any other signals. This time, however, through all the crackle and static came a voice she knew well. It was Chief Tariri transmitting on a Wycliffe radio from his hut in Peru!

"Come quickly," Rachel called to the group, who all appeared in seconds. "Listen. This is Tariri, the chief Dayuma met across the great waters."

The crowd hunched in closer to listen to his words.

"What is he saying Nimu?" Dawa asked.

Rachel listened carefully. Although she could not recall all of the Shapra dialect, she recalled enough of it to piece together what the chief was saying. "He is telling someone, 'Since I believed in Jesus I live well. Instead of killing, I try to love and help everyone, even my enemies.'"

The airwaves went dead, but the impression left from actually hearing Chief Tariri's voice was electrifying. For the next two or three days, Rachel heard many people asking each other, "Did you hear what the headhunting chief said on Nimu's talking machine?"

Then on the fourth morning Dawa came to Rachel. "Uncle Gikita is now like Tariri. Talking to God, he walks to and fro in the forest," she said.

Rachel wept privately, overwhelmed with the spiritual changes that were beginning to take place around her.

That Sunday Dayuma challenged everyone. "When the foreigners get together, they ask those who know for sure that God has made their heart clean to tell each other. Who among us will speak what God has done in his heart?"

Dawa spoke up. "I did not live well before. But now I love God with all my heart."

After a period of silence, Dyuwi began counting on his fingers. "I killed this one, and this one, and this one." As Rachel looked on, she knew that one of the fingers represented Dyuwi's part in killing Nate and the other four men. "That was before I knew Jesus. Now He has cleaned my heart," Dyuwi finished.

Kimo, who was also one of the killers, interrupted. "Jesus' blood washed my heart clean. Loving Him, I now live."

No one else spoke up, but that was certainly enough excitement that morning for Rachel, Betty, and Dayuma.

Later in the day, as Rachel was writing in her journal, Nimonga came to visit her. He was a third member of the killing party at Palm Beach. Rachel chose her words carefully as she spoke to him. "Nimonga, did you understand God's Carvings this morning when Dayuma spoke about God forgiving sins?"

"Yes," he replied.

"And will you say yes to God?"

"I will," Nimonga replied.

Gikita was the next man to seek Rachel out. He tried to count how many people he had killed in his lifetime but became frustrated when he ran out of fingers and toes. "Not knowing God, I did not do well," he said. Rachel was touched to see that Gikita had tears in his eyes. "Now, knowing God, I will do better."

A week later, the fifth killer, Minkayi, confessed his desire to become a Christian. "Believing, I am now walking Jesus' trail to the sky," he announced jubilantly one Sunday morning.

Not long after this, Rachel received a startling radio message. "The president of Ecuador is coming to Limoncocha, and he wants to meet some Aucas at an official ceremony," the voice on the other end of the radio announced. Rachel knew that it would be rude not to show up, and she wondered which members of Dayuma's clan to take to visit such an important man. Eventually she decided to take Dayuma, Kimo, and Dawa. Together the four of them walked the trail to Arajuno, where they were picked up by a JAARS airplane and flown to Limoncocha. Rachel observed with amusement as Kimo sat with his face pressed hard against the airplane window throughout the flight, watching the jungle pass beneath him.

The JAARS plane arrived at Limoncocha just ahead of the two official airplanes from Quito carrying President Velasco Ibarra and his entourage, among them Uncle Cam, who had flown in from North Carolina for the ceremony.

Representatives came from each tribe in Ecuador that Wycliffe Bible Translators was working among. Rachel guided Kimo and Dawa to their place in the crowd gathered for the official ceremony. Just as the ceremony was about to get under way, rain began to pour down, and the formal introductory ceremony had to be canceled. But Rachel soon learned that President Ibarra did not mind too much. In fact, he was really only interested in meeting members of the fearsome Auca tribe, and soon Rachel, Dayuma, Kimo, and Dawa were led into a building for a private meeting with the president.

"Mr. President, may I present Miss Rachel Saint. You met her several years ago when a group of SIL workers came to your residence to be presented to you," Uncle Cam began.

President Ibarra nodded slightly to acknowledge that he remembered the occasion.

"And this is Dayuma," Uncle Cam went on. "She is a young Auca Miss Saint found working at a hacienda in the Oriente."

Uncle Cam was about to continue the introduction when Kimo cut him short. He suddenly stepped forward and rubbed his hand over the president's bald head.

Rachel could feel her cheeks turn bright red with embarrassment. "Please excuse him, Mr. President. He must be swatting a bug," Rachel sputtered by way of apology.

"I don't think he's ever seen a bald head before, and he wants to know if it's real," Uncle Cam interjected.

Everyone laughed, even the president, who reassured Rachel that he was not offended by Kimo's action.

Finally Kimo and Dawa squatted on the floor, and Dayuma sat on a low stool nearby, keeping a careful eye on them lest Kimo do anything else that might embarrass Rachel or insult President Ibarra.

The meeting continued. President Ibarra wanted to know how Rachel and Betty had been able to pacify the dangerous Auca killers.

"We give all the credit and glory to God, Mr. President," Rachel said. "He is the One who arranged all of the circumstances for us to safely enter their territory." Rachel went on to tell the president more of the specific details about the events that had led up to her and Betty's going to live among the Waorani. She also filled him in on Kimo's and Dawa's backgrounds.

"So this man is one of those who killed the missionaries," the president said rhetorically, pointing to Kimo. "And the other four involved in that attack have also stopped killing. How did this happen?"

Rachel explained to the president how the same message of forgiveness and faith in Jesus Christ to change a person's heart serves all people everywhere.

"But what can this man comprehend of God?" President Ibarra asked, once again pointing to Kimo.

"Why don't you ask him? I will translate for you," Rachel responded.

"Very well," the president replied. Then addressing Kimo, he asked, "Who is Jesus Christ, Kimo?"

Rachel translated his words. Kimo thought about them for a moment as a broad smile spread across his face. "He is the One who came from heaven and died for my sins. He is the One who made me stop killing. Now I live happily with my brothers."

When Kimo had finished speaking, Rachel translated his words for the president.

Rachel watched as President Ibarra shook his head in amazement. "Amazing, simply amazing," the president said.

The following morning Uncle Cam told Rachel that the president had talked about the change in Kimo all through dinner the night before. President Ibarra was impressed with the work of Wycliffe in his country and was particularly fascinated with the work Rachel had undertaken among the Waorani.

After three days at Limoncocha, Rachel, Dayuma, Kimo, and Dawa were flown back to Arajuno, from where they trudged back into Waorani territory. Kimo had been most impressed with the airplane ride from Arajuno to Limoncocha and back, and as they walked, he talked to Rachel about building a landing strip at the settlement beside the Tiwaeno River. Of course it would be a daunting task to carve a six-hundred-foot strip out of the virgin jungle, but Rachel assured Kimo that she thought it would be a good thing to do.

Back at the settlement, everyone else thought an airstrip where a wood-bee could land might be a good thing, but everyone also recognized the enormity of the task. Rachel received some unexpected help, however, in encouraging the tribe to start work on the project. A successful hunting expedition had just returned with many wild pigs the hunters had speared. But since the Waorani had no way to preserve meat, the pigs would have to be eaten quickly. Rachel talked the women into preparing a series of feasts for any man who would help clear the landing strip. The idea was a huge success, and everyone soon joined in in clearing the jungle. Rachel was amazed at the progress the workers quickly made. Every now and then she would pause from her digging and clearing and watch the group of Waoranis working together. As she did so, her thoughts went back to Nate. How she wished he were alive to see such a scene.

When the airstrip was finished, Rachel, Betty, and Dayuma talked among themselves about the safety of a pilot flying into the village. Few of the Waoranis had had any contact with the outside world, other than Rachel and Betty, and they were still deeply suspicious of outsiders. Bringing a white man into the village in an airplane concerned Rachel. Would the people attack the plane and strip it as they had done to Nate's plane at Palm Beach? Would one of them secretly make plans to spear the pilot? No one knew for sure. The three women prayed about the situation, and they felt that the time was right to invite Don Smith, the JAARS pilot in the area, to land his plane on the new airstrip.

It was an historic moment as the airplane slipped below tree level and touched down on the new landing strip. Rachel and Dayuma hugged and laughed as Don waved to everyone from the cockpit.

Don delivered supplies and mail to Rachel and Betty, and then Dyuwi offered a prayer in honor of the occasion. "Our Father in Heaven, we thank You for bringing this day when our people and outsiders can meet together in peace," he prayed.

Rachel said a big amen to his prayer.

As she watched the airplane take off, Rachel imagined all the ways the new airstrip would help the Waorani. They were now a mere ten minutes by air from Arajuno, thirty from Shell Mera, and thirty from Limoncocha. Now a sick Waorani could be at the medical clinic at Shell Mera in a matter of minutes, not the days it would take slogging through the jungle to get there.

The JAARS airplane soon became an indispensable part of life at the Tiwaeno settlement. Other than Don Smith, the pilot, the first "outside" visitor to be flown in was Catherine Peeke, who had come to Ecuador with Rachel and had accompanied Rachel to Hacienda Ila, where they first met Dayuma. Catherine and fellow Wycliffe worker Mary Sargent had come to Ecuador wanting to translate the Bible into the Záparo language but, after a long and extensive search, had found only ten Záparo speakers in the country. Western diseases had all but killed off the once robust Záparo Indians. After learning that the number of Záparo Indians was so few, Catherine was now in search of a new tribe to work among. In the meantime, she told Rachel, she was studying for her doctorate in linguistics at the University of Indiana and planned to write her dissertation on Waorani grammar. Hearing this made Rachel very happy. Grammar was Rachel's most difficult area of language study, and she welcomed Catherine's insights and advice.

Another visitor to the settlement was Dr. Everett Fuller from the medical clinic at Shell Mera. Dr.

Fuller came to Tiwaeno to hold a health clinic among the people of the settlement. Dayuma was very excited when she heard that the doctor was coming. "Can he enter the believers in the water?" she asked Rachel.

Rachel agreed that it would be a good idea to ask whether anyone wanted to be baptized. Dawa, Kimo, Komi, Nimonga, Gimari, Gikita, and three other adults all indicated that they were ready to take that step. It was a wonderful day for Rachel. In describing the event in a letter to her parents she wrote, "For me—one who has watched the expression of Auca faces turn from resentment to friendship, from unbelief to belief—the biggest blessing was to see the sweet radiance of their faces as they came up from the waters. Our hearts rejoiced in this answer to the sacrifice and the prayers of many people."

The baptism was quickly followed by another Christian ceremony—a wedding. Dayuma and Komi were married with all the usual Waorani celebration, with the addition of some new traditions—prayer and a short sermon.

Soon after Dayuma's wedding, Betty announced that she and Valerie would soon be leaving the village. Based on personality, Catherine was a much better fit with Rachel, so Betty had decided to leave so that Catherine could take her place and become Rachel's permanent partner. The transition was made, though Rachel soon found herself alone at Tiwaeno for some time when Catherine returned to the United States to finish studying for her doctorate.

Still, there was plenty to keep Rachel busy. By now the nucleus of believers at the settlement had built themselves a thatched church—God's speaking-house—where each evening they held meetings, which Rachel attended. The translation work was also moving ahead. At times it felt to Rachel that she was making fast progress, and at other times she wished that Catherine would hurry back to speed things along.

When news arrived that her eighty-four-year-old father had died, Rachel did not feel that she could go home for the funeral. A new danger was looming. Big oil companies, including Texaco and Gulf Oil, were flying airplanes overhead, surveying the Curaray River basin from the air. Rachel knew that this could mean only one thing: they were preparing to invade the jungle once again in a quest for black gold—oil.

Chapter 15

The Downriver People

In January 1964 news of a new Waorani attack spread around the world. This time the attackers were not Dayuma's immediate relatives but their distant downriver cousins, who lived along the Napo River. Rachel could only guess at their motives for the attack, but it seemed fairly certain that it had to do with the twenty-seven oil companies now vying for rights to drill for oil in the Oriente.

Although their own lands were threatened, Dayuma and her clan were greatly concerned about what might happen to their downriver kin. They realized that if the downriver people were not reached with the gospel soon, they would continue their attacks on foreigners. It would then be only a matter of time before the big oil companies lost patience with them and killed all of the downriver tribe.

In response to this escalating situation, Gikita and Dyuwi wanted to visit the downriver tribe and tell them about Jesus. Rachel felt, however, that this would be an unsafe course of action, and she prayed hard that God would open up some other way to make contact. Her prayers were answered in the form of a radio message from a remote jungle settlement. The settler on the radio informed Rachel that he had shot a teenage girl. She was seriously injured and had been wearing nothing but a string around her waist and big balsa wood earplugs. Rachel knew immediately that the girl must be a Waorani, and she radioed Shell Mera for a plane to come and pick her up and take her to the remote settlement.

When Rachel arrived at the outpost, the teenage girl was running a high temperature and looked very scared. She whimpered when Rachel came near her. Rachel could see that the settler and his wife had bandaged her side where the bullets had entered, but blood was seeping through the bandage.

"Two bullets," the settler said. "We came across her and a man in a canoe. The man threw spears at us, and we shot back."

"Let me alone to talk with the girl," Rachel said.

The settler and his wife nodded and left the room.

"My name is Nimu," Rachel said soothingly in Waorani. "Father God sent me to live with your people in Tiwaeno. Dayuma is my adopted sister."

"Dayuma!" the girl exclaimed as she tried to sit up. "Dayuma lives? I thought the outsiders shot her and ate her many seasons ago. They shot me. Are they going to eat me now?"

"No one is going to eat you," Rachel replied as she pulled a thermometer from her bag. "We all live in peace at Tiwaeno, and we want you all to come and live with us. What is your name?"

"Oncaye," the girl answered. "Titada is my mother."

Rachel nodded. "Now put this under your tongue," she said. "It is not going to hurt you."

Oncaye obediently opened her mouth, and Rachel inserted the thermometer under her tongue. The mercury rose to 102 degrees.

Rachel walked outside and spoke to the MAF pilot who had flown her to the remote outpost. "If there's any chance of saving her life, we have to get her back to the hospital at Shell Mera and get those bullets out," she said.

The pilot sprang into action, and soon Oncaye was taking her first airplane ride.

At Shell Mera the medical staff were able to safely remove the bullets from Oncaye's side, and Oncaye began a long period of recovery. As she began to feel stronger, Oncaye told Rachel more about her life. As it turned out, she had four older sisters who had fled the tribe years before and whom she thought were long dead. Rachel had the joy of telling her that all four of her sisters, including Dawa, were alive and safe and living at Tiwaeno. Rachel quickly sent a plane to Tiwaeno to collect Oncaye's sisters and bring them back to Shell Mera so that Oncaye could see them for herself.

The sisters were astonished when they arrived at Shell Mera and came face-to-face with Oncaye.

They talked excitedly among themselves, and the conversation soon shifted to how the hearts of the Tiwaeno Waoranis had changed after hearing God's Carvings.

When Oncaye was well enough, Rachel took her back to Tiwaeno, where everyone welcomed her warmly.

"We do not kill our babies when they cry," the people there told her. "Doing well, we speak of the God who made the world."

Gikita was moved when he heard Oncaye's stories, especially when she told how her people were planning to attack the oil workers.

"We must go to them soon," Gikita said. "They must hear God's Carvings before they die."

In February 1965 four Waoranis—Dyuwi, Tona, Oncaye, and her sister Boika—set out from Tiwaeno to find their downriver relatives. Seven days later they were back at Tiwaeno. Oncaye reported that her bullet wounds had opened up again and a tree had fallen on Tona's leg, making it impossible for them to go on.

Still, the group decided that another attempt to reach the downriver people should be made. Dyuwi, Minkayi, and Gikita, three of the Palm Beach killers, set out. This time, though, torrential rain and subsequent flooding turned them back. Their arrival back in Tiwaeno was a bitter blow to the Christians there, and the three men resolved to set out again as soon as possible to reach the downriver people.

In the meantime Rachel had finished translating the book of Mark into Waorani. Proudly she sent the translation off to Mexico City, where the American Bible Society had promised to print it. The first shipment of the printed copies of Mark's gospel was flown into Tiwaeno on Good Friday 1965. Accompanying the precious cargo on the airplane were Philip and Steve Saint, Nate's two sons, now aged eleven and fourteen.

Rachel was as delighted to see her nephews as she was the newly printed Gospel of Mark. A jubilant dedication service was held on Easter Sunday. Of course, Rachel now realized that with the Gospel printed in Waorani, her next challenge was to teach the people to read.

Soon after Easter, sixteen-year-old Kathy Saint arrived at Tiwaeno. She wanted to be baptized and asked Rachel if a Waorani Christian elder could baptize her. Rachel spoke to the members of the church about it, and everyone agreed that it was a great idea. Then Steve, a teenage boy named Iniwa, and Oncaye asked to be baptized.

Marj Saint flew in from Quito to witness the baptism, and on June 25 a large group of people set out from Tiwaeno for Palm Beach. Kimo and Dyuwi led the way. The following day the group gathered on the edge of the Curaray River at Palm Beach. They stood beside the grave of the five martyred missionary men as Kimo, Kathy and Steve Saint, Oncaye, and Iniwa waded into the river. The crowd sang "We Rest in Thee," which had been the five dead men's favorite hymn. When they had finished singing, Rachel looked up and saw five red jungle flowers. For her they symbolized Nate and the other four men who had given their lives so that such an event as the baptism might one day take place among the Waorani.

After the final bars of the hymn faded away, Kimo baptized each of the four candidates one after the other. When he was finished, he asked the people to bow their heads while he prayed. "Father in heaven," he began, "You know that we have sinned here. We were ignorant. We did not know that our brothers had come to tell us about You. But now You have put our sins in the deepest water, and happily we serve You and know we will see again those that we killed. Father God, these young brothers and sisters have entered into the water. Help them to live happily, as we do. Help them to be true to You and Your Carvings. Amen."

By the time Kimo had finished praying, tears were streaming down Rachel's cheeks. Once again she wished that Nate could have been there to witness the scene. Yet she knew that it was his death and the death of the other four that had paved the way for the baptism she had just witnessed. And she knew that Nate would have been touched by the fact that Kimo, one of the killers, was the man who conducted the baptism.

The next visitors to Tiwaeno arrived in November 1965. They were Dr. Raymond Edman from Wheaton College and his wife. They came to hold the first ever Waorani Bible conference. On the last day of the conference, Dr. Edman read from Acts 13 about Paul and Barnabas being sent off as missionaries. Then he challenged those present to renew their dedication to reach their downriver neighbors. Dyuwi, Tona, and Oncaye all came to the altar at the end of the service to pray for strength and courage to go to the downriver people.

Rachel knew how important it was to get to the downriver Waorani as soon as possible. The oil-drilling situation was becoming more menacing with each passing week. Oil workers were encroaching more and more into Waorani territory, and plans were under way to crisscross the Oriente with pipelines.

Don Smith, the JAARS pilot, kept Rachel up to date with any Waorani sightings, and in February 1966 he reported seeing a settlement. He flew into Tiwaeno and picked up Dyuwi, Dayuma, and Oncaye so that they, too, could see the settlement from the air. When they got back, Oncaye was breathless with excitement. "Swooping down low, I saw my mother."

Dayuma was more sober. "A very big man threw spears at the plane," she reported.

Even so, finding the exact location of a downriver group was enough to spur the Tiwaeno Waorani into action. Within a few days, Dyuwi, Tona, Oncaye, and her sister Boika set out on foot for the settlement. They carried a few supplies with them and a radio to keep in contact with Rachel and Don. The plan was for Don to keep an eye on the settlement and guide the four Waorani missionaries to it if they strayed off course.

Several days later the four came bursting back into Tiwaeno, shaken to the core. Rachel listened as Oncaye recounted what happened.

"We had walked for several days," she said, "when we saw some footprints. They belonged to my family, and we followed them. As we walked, we noticed dark stains on the ground beside the footprints. It was nearly dark when we came to a small hut. The smell was very bad, and the hut was filled with buzzards. We crept forward, and inside we found the body of my mother with spears protruding from her. I screamed, and we ran. We ran for a long time, and it was very dark before we stopped and lit a fire. Dyuwi and Tona were tired, and so they slept while Boika and I prepared some food. But soon we both knew there were spies in the jungle watching us. I looked at Boika, and we both began to talk about Father God. Then I heard the quiet whistle from the jungle, the signal of my people to attack. I called to the men in the jungle and said, 'You plan to kill me, too? Very well, go ahead and try. You cannot hurt me. You will just kill my body. My soul will go to be with Father God.' By then Dyuwi and Tona were awake, and we began to run as fast as we could through the jungle toward Tiwaeno. But the downriver men were following our footprints. So I prayed, 'God, make it rain. Hurry!' And soon it began to pour and wash away our footprints so that the men could not follow us."

Rachel breathed deeply. It was a harrowing story, and the four had been lucky to escape. Rachel also felt deep compassion for Oncaye's having to see the speared, decaying body of her dead mother. Things may have changed among the upriver people at Tiwaeno, but not so for the downriver Waorani. Yet God had opened the way with Dayuma's clan, and Rachel was sure that He would do the same with the downriver people.

As Rachel worked on at Tiwaeno, the world outside was commemorating the ten-year anniversary of the deaths of the five missionaries at Palm Beach. The government of Ecuador issued postage stamps, each with a likeness of one of the five murdered men, and Dr. Edman wrote a series of articles for Christian magazines. The Billy Graham organization distributed over one hundred thousand copies of a pamphlet Rachel had written called *Ten Years After the Massacre.* All of the attention on the deaths of the men renewed interest in the Waorani, and in mid-1966 Cameron Townsend contacted Rachel on the radio. He had one request—bring two Waorani Christians and come to the World Congress of Evangelism in Berlin, Germany, in November.

Rachel was reluctant to leave the jungle, but once again she deferred to Uncle Cam's judgment. She picked Kimo and Dayuma's husband, Komi, to accompany her to Berlin. The first leg of their journey took them to Huntingdon Valley to visit Rachel's aging mother. It was the first time Kimo and Komi had ever left the jungle, and their reaction to the outside world provided Rachel with many humorous moments. When they got off the airplane in

Quito to catch their plane to the United States, Kimo saw a truck. "Look, there is an airplane walking!" he exclaimed.

In Huntingdon Valley Rachel outfitted the two Waorani men in suitable winter attire. And when Kimo and Komi emerged wearing suits, overcoats, dress shoes, scarves, and hats, she found it hard to hold back the laughter. The two men who had spent most of their lives going naked looked so different. Of course, getting dress shoes to fit their wide feet had not been easy, and it had taken them both a little while to get used to wearing the heavy shoes. After Kimo and Komi had received some dental work, they set out with Rachel for Berlin.

In Berlin the two Waorani men were most impressed with the cave (hotel) they stayed in. They found it hard to believe that such a big building for people to sleep in existed. However, both of them were perturbed when Rachel took them to a park and they could not find one monkey in the trees. After considering the situation for some time, Kimo explained, "It is because the trees are too short and too far apart for monkeys to jump from one treetop to the next."

The number of people attending the World Congress of Evangelism also impressed the men. "We did not know God's believing family was so big," they told Rachel.

Kimo and Komi were a huge hit at the congress. Wherever they went, crowds gathered around them to finally catch a glimpse of one of the Aucas they had heard so much about.

On the second-to-last day of the congress, Kimo and Komi got to stand before the gathered crowd and speak while Rachel translated for them. To help the flow of their presentation, George Cowan, one of the Wycliffe leaders, asked a number of questions. His final question to Kimo was "Do you have a message for the believers here who come from all over the world?"

Staring out across the nearly twelve hundred people gathered in the hall, Kimo replied, "I say to you, take God's Carving to all the people in your land. We will go home and take God's message to our downriver enemies. We will say to them, 'Believing in God and His Son Jesus, we live well. We have stopped spearing and choking babies. We live happily with our families.' This we will say and invite them to believe in God and live in peace with us."

When Rachel had finished interpreting his words, the crowd broke out into a huge round of applause.

Following the close of the World Congress of Evangelism in Berlin, Rachel, Kimo, and Komi toured several European cities. One of the cities they visited was London. It was an emotional moment for Rachel as she arrived there. Rachel had not visited London since she was eighteen years old, when she had come with Mrs. Parmalee. It was on that trip, aboard the ship returning to the United States from London, that Rachel had had the vision of a group of people in the jungle beckoning to her to come to them. They were "her" people, the people she felt certain God was leading her to. And now, all these years later, she was in London again with two members of that very tribe.

Finally, after six weeks away, the three of them arrived back at Tiwaeno. Everyone was anxious to hear about all that Kimo and Komi had seen and done. To Rachel's surprise, it was not the tall buildings, ribbons of highways, ships, or large airplanes the men had seen that impressed them but rather the sheer number of people they had encountered.

"Look at all the trees around us," Kimo told those who had gathered to hear about the trip. "Look as far as you can see. Beyond the hills and mountains there are more trees. Think of all the leaves on all those trees. That is how many foreigners there are."

Rachel had barely settled back into the routine of jungle life when news came of another Waorani killing, this time of a Quichua man on the Napo River. Again the need to reach the downriver people loomed, but no one was sure how to go about it. Then at Christmas Don Smith suggested to Rachel that they use Nate's spiral-line method to lower a radio receiver and transmitter to the group. That way Oncaye could talk to them and prepare them to receive upriver guests.

Everything was meticulously prepared. A transmitter was placed in the bottom of a basket, and Don and Oncaye flew off to deliver it. While they were gone, Rachel and Gikita led a prayer meeting in Tiwaeno. They prayed fervently that this time the mission would be successful.

When the airplane finally touched down again at the settlement, Oncaye jumped out. "I talked to my brother Tyaento!" she shouted. "He is going to meet me at Moipa's field in two days. He wants me to bring an ax."

Everyone at Tiwaeno—and no one more than Rachel Saint—hoped that Oncaye was not walking into a trap.

Chapter 16

The Years Go By

Oncaye, Dawa, Kimo, and Dyuwi set off down the trail to go and meet Oncaye's family. Rachel waited anxiously by the radio for any reports on how the four were getting on. Finally, three days after they had set out, the radio crackled to life. It was Oncaye, and her report brought tears to Rachel's eyes. Excitedly Oncaye reported how her mother had welcomed the group. Apparently the badly decayed body they had discovered on their previous trip turned out to be that of Oncaye's cousin and not her mother. Soon other members of Oncaye's family filtered into the clearing in the jungle to see their long-lost relatives.

Dawa also spoke to Rachel. She, too, was excited to see her relatives, but she explained that Oncaye's sister-in-law Wina was seriously ill from a poisonous snakebite. In fact, Wina had been left to die in her hammock, but Dawa had been able to give her a shot of serum from her medical kit and pray for her. After listening to the report, Rachel felt that Wina would need more medical care, so she encouraged Dawa and the others to bring Wina back to Tiwaeno.

Wina agreed to let Kimo carry her back over the trail to her upriver relatives. It took seven days of toil to get Wina back to Tiwaeno, but she arrived alive and accompanied by ten other members of Oncaye's family. The Tiwaeno Christians welcomed Oncaye's relatives, and before long most of the newcomers had become Christians themselves.

The people still had much concern, though, for the many other splinter groups of downriver people. No one knew exactly how many there were, but in June 1968, Oncaye and her mother set out to find them. This time it was not difficult. Their old downriver enemies were weak from exposure to the flu. Many of the people could hardly walk, and they welcomed an invitation to return to Tiwaeno, where they could get medical help.

Rachel greeted the first small group of flu-ridden downriver people to arrive back with Oncaye and her mother. She radioed the hospital at Shell Mera for advice on how best to treat them. Other small groups of downriver people began straggling into the village.

By the time Rachel could count the influx of people, she realized that ninety-three newcomers were among them. Including the eleven members of

Oncaye's family who had already joined them, the total number of new arrivals at Tiwaeno was 104, exactly matching the population that, in the ten years Rachel had lived there, had grown from 56 to 104 people.

Every resource the community had was stretched as far as it would go. The healthy Tiwaeno men hunted for twice as many people as before, and the women walked farther in search of bananas and overgrown yucca gardens. Rachel was proud of the way the Christians in the community were reaching out to their old enemies, but she was also concerned about what would happen when the downriver men regained their strength. The men were hardened killers who probably thought that feeding an enemy was a sign of weakness.

The Tiwaeno Christians did all they could to make sure their guests knew about their change of heart. "Here we do not kill others," they announced. "Nor do we take a wife's sister or any other woman who does not want to be our wife. We obey God's Carvings. Happily and peacefully we live, believing in the God who made us all."

On the whole, despite several flare-ups, the downriver people behaved well while they lived in Tiwaeno. As they began to recover their strength after their bout with influenza, several of the men cleared land a few miles away and built their own village.

The next challenge Rachel faced was something more serious than the flu—polio. The first case of the disease, that of a downriver Waorani, was diagnosed on the same day, September 2, 1969, that Rachel learned that her mother had died. Rachel hardly had time to mourn the passing of Katherine Saint. She was too overwhelmed with the nursing task that was quickly overtaking her and the other Christians at Tiwaeno.

The downriver people were still accustomed to thinking that illness and death were the result of curses, and so when they started getting ill, they looked around for someone to blame. Rachel found herself grabbing newly whittled spears and smashing them over her knee, defying anyone to commit a spearing in the village. Her tactics worked, though the toll from the polio virus was devastating. By the time the disease had run its course, fourteen people were dead, and nine others were in critical condition.

The doctors at the hospital in Shell Mera took in the nine polio patients and made manually operated iron lungs to keep them alive. Medical charities from Wheaton College sent crutches and wheelchairs for the disabled, and nurses and physical therapists arrived to help with rehabilitation. Despite their best efforts, two more patients died.

One of the nurses assigned to help with the polio outbreak in Tiwaeno itself was Rosi Jung, from Germany. Rachel loved Rosi's quiet, efficient manner from the start, and Rosi soon signed on as a permanent helper to Rachel. She joined Catherine, who had now completed her doctorate and was permanently assigned to work among the Waorani tribe.

With three workers, a lot more work was able to get done. Rachel and her two helpers focused their attention on literacy, and soon a believer named Tona began to shine academically. Rachel encouraged him to become a teacher, and Tona took up the challenge of helping his people learn to read and write.

Rachel and the others at Tiwaeno estimated that at least two hundred other Waoranis were living in the jungle. They named one of the bands the "ridge people."

When word arrived that the oil workers were preparing to clear the ridge, Tona, who thought that his sister Omade lived with the ridge people, felt he had to do something. He asked a helicopter pilot for one of the oil companies to parachute him down onto the ridge. It was a daring plan. Rachel was concerned that it would fail, depriving Tiwaeno of its best reader and teacher. But Tona assured her that God was calling him to take the gospel to the ridge people.

After Tona left on his mission, Rachel kept in touch with him by radio. Much to her relief, everything seemed to be going well. Tona reported that he had found both his sister and his brother and that they had both welcomed him. Each morning Tona relayed his progress to Rachel. The group was listening to his teaching from God's Carvings, and several people were interested in going back to meet the believers at Tiwaeno.

Then, on June 5, 1970, Tona reported to Rachel that the group was planning a big party nearby. At first Tona thought it would be safer to remove himself from the situation, but after praying all night, he said that he felt he should stay and preach to them all.

One day passed, and then the next. The radio was silent. Catherine and Dawa were flown over the clearing where the party had been held to see if they could spot Tona. All they saw was that the huts in the area had been burned to the ground. No one knew what had happened to Tona, but Rachel was sure that he would find a way to contact her soon if he was alive.

In the meantime Rachel received word that Wycliffe Associates, a group of Wycliffe supporters, wanted her to go on a tour of the United States to raise awareness of Wycliffe's mission. The Wycliffe supporters suggested that she bring several of the Waorani Christians with her. As was usually the case, Rachel did not want to go. She was worried about Tona and the unreached Waoranis wandering the ridge country. But Wycliffe Associates was very persistent, and eventually Rachel agreed to take Kimo, Dawa, Gikita, and Dayuma's son Sam with her. When they left in the spring of 1971, they still had no news of Tona.

The Auca Update Rallies held across the United States were far more popular and exhausting than Rachel could ever have imagined. For two months the group was flown from city to city. Rachel or Sam, who was now a well-educated young man, interpreted for the others in the many crusades they spoke at and the television shows they appeared on. At times it seemed to Rachel that everyone in America knew who they were, and although she did her best to shield the others from overexposure to the media, it was almost impossible.

At one stage Dawa became ill, and Rachel questioned whether or not it was all worth it. The only reason she continued with the tour to the end was that many people commented to her and other Wycliffe workers that the testimonies of the Waorani Christians had challenged them to go out as missionaries.

By the time the group arrived back in the Oriente, Rachel, who was fifty-seven years old by now, was on the verge of a nervous collapse. It did not take much for Catherine and Rosi to convince her that she needed to take a break. For the first time in many years, Rachel returned to the United States alone.

While in the United States, Rachel received a letter from Catherine with the sad news that Tona had been speared by his relatives. The relatives had told Dyuwi that Tona's last words were, "You may kill me, but I am not afraid. I will only go to heaven."

As she received the news, Rachel was sure that this first Waorani martyr was in heaven with her brother and her parents.

While in the United States, Rachel had to face the fact that she was having problems seeing. Her eyes had developed cataracts, and something had to be done about them. Rachel underwent successful surgery on her right eye to remove the cataract.

However, she did not stay home long enough to have the left eye operated on. Rachel felt that she did not have the time to wait for the second operation. She had to get back to her people, who needed her now more than ever.

About ten years earlier, the oil companies and the government of Ecuador had gotten together and decided to draw a line around Waorani lands. They called it a protectorate, but it reminded Rachel of the Indian reservations in the United States. The protectorate consisted of forty thousand acres of land, one tenth of the traditional Waorani territory, and it conferred on the Waorani no mineral rights to the oil that was under their land. The size of the protectorate was far too small for the Waoranis to roam so that they could hunt, fish, and gather enough fruit and vegetables to live on. At first the small amount of land had not been a problem, because the oil companies did not patrol the borders of the protectorate and the Waoranis wandered far outside it to hunt. But now things were changing. The land itself was changing too. Settlers on the edges of the protectorate hunted with guns and fished with commercial nets, dramatically reducing the number of animals and fish. Worse still, many of the oil companies were using dynamite and DDT in the area. Soon some streams and rivers had no fish left in them at all.

All of this was new and unbelievable to the Waorani. For as long as the people could remember, the jungle had always produced enough game and plants for them to eat and use to make their huts. But now, right before their eyes, the things they needed to keep their culture alive were disappearing, and no one on the outside seemed to care.

Rachel returned to the Oriente to do whatever she could about the situation. When she arrived at Tiwaeno, she found Patricia Kelly, a new Wycliffe worker, living there. Patricia had been assigned to build a better literacy program. This was the job Rachel had been training Tona to do, but now that Tona was dead, someone had to help the people learn to read and write.

Rachel saw other changes in the area as well. The Plymouth Brethren Church had sent in a missionary who had started a school and church for Quichua Indians right on the edge of the protectorate. Many of the Waorani believers began attending the school, breaking up the close-knit complexity of the Christian community that had thrived in Tiwaeno.

Rachel reeled at all the changes. Whether she liked it or not, life would not be the same. The next change came when Wycliffe sent another couple into the area: Dr. Jim Yost and his wife, Kathie. The Yosts were assigned to undertake an anthropological survey, a study of how the Waoranis lived. What they found confirmed what Rachel had always known—before Christianity came, the Waoranis had lived violent and short lives.

Jim Yost interviewed the people. In asking them questions that spanned six generations, he discovered that 61 percent of Waoranis had died from being speared, 13 percent had been shot by outsiders, 12 percent had died from illness, 4 percent had died from snakebites, 4 percent were babies and children who had been buried alive, and 6 percent had died of unknown causes.

In 1976 a team of six scientists from Duke University joined in the survey. It seemed to Rachel as if the whole world suddenly wanted to know how a Stone-Age jungle tribe was adjusting to the encroaching modern world. The scientists found that the Waorani had contracted some new diseases, including scabies and various lung diseases brought in from the outside. Some of the transfer of the diseases into the tribe was occurring because Waorani men were seeking employment in the oil fields. In 1977 ten Waorani men worked for oil companies; a year later there were thirty Waorani workers. The influx of money into the Waorani villages changed the people even more. Now the Waorani had to learn how to work for cash and spend it wisely. They were often taken advantage of because they could not count to high numbers and did not know how much an item was worth.

In traditional Waorani culture, everything had always been shared among tribal members. But now that outside merchandise was coming in, things were different. For the first time, Waoranis wanted to own their own things. Radios, clothes, and blowguns became coveted items and led to arguments and fights.

All of these factors led Jim Yost to write a startling report to the leaders of Wycliffe Bible Translators.

At least it was startling to Rachel, and her eyes widened as she read:

> Withdraw SIL workers from the protectorate for a time so that the Waorani can learn better to stand alone. Upon returning, workers should spread out among the settlements and not concentrate in Tiwaeno. More translation should be done in Limoncocha with Waorani assistants....
>
> Stop the migration from the ridge, at least until more land could be secured and newcomers could fend for themselves without becoming dependent on relatives in the protectorate.

For the first time in many years, Rachel was faced with the fact that Wycliffe viewed her as a temporary worker in the tribe, someone who could be recalled at any time. In her nearly twenty years of living among the Waorani, twelve of them alone, Rachel had come to see herself as one of them, not as an outsider. The Waorani were "her people," and she wept to think of leaving them.

In the end, however, Rachel bowed to the wishes of Wycliffe leadership and removed herself from the tribe. She did not tell anyone how long she would be gone, because she did not know herself. Besides, she needed to leave for a short while anyway; her eyes were getting weaker to the point where she was almost blind. It was time for another operation.

With a heavy heart, Rachel climbed aboard a JAARS airplane that taxied down the runway that she had helped to build with her own hands. A hundred Waorani faces stared back at her as the plane gathered speed. Many of the people had tears streaming down their faces as the plane lifted off the ground. It was the most wrenching time Rachel could ever recall in her life.

Rachel flew to Quito and then on to Florida, where she had two successful eye operations. At sixty-five years of age she was feeling fit and well again and was ready to go home to Tiwaeno. She knew, however, that she could not. Instead she returned to Quito to live in a room at the Wycliffe/SIL headquarters. Rachel continued to want to go home to Tiwaeno but contented herself with working hard at her Bible translation work. In an interview with a biographer, she confided, "Twenty years ago I started out to translate the Bible into Auca. I've been sidetracked by helping the people. It seems I helped them too well, at the sacrifice of my prime work. My translations are way behind. People who started in other languages in other parts of the world years after me have long finished. Now I have to get my priorities right. I have to finish the work I started out to do, the work Nate and the others died for."

Age did not make Rachel any more tactful, either. When the biographer reminded her that some people thought the Waorani would be better off if she had never gone into the tribe, she retorted, "Don't believe it. There is no way that the Auca were going to be left alone. That is a lovely fairy story thought up by preservationists. With oilmen and settlers in the jungle, there would have been a bloodbath, and I know who would have come off the worst. Within a decade there would have been no Aucas and no language to preserve. These so-called do-gooders just don't know what they're talking about.... How many of them have been in the jungle for more than a week, if that, and studied the problems? They fly in, do a lightning so-called investigation, then fly out, talking nonsense. You have to live in the jungle and live with the day-to-day problems to know what the problems are."

Rachel did return to the jungle briefly in June 1992 to mark the presentation of the entire New Testament in the Waorani language. All of her translation partners through the years, including Mary Sargent and Catherine Peeke, were there. The Saint clan turned out in large numbers too. Rachel was proud to show eight of her nieces and nephews Palm Beach and Tiwaeno, where she had spent so much of her life.

A new settlement named Tonampade (Tona's village) had sprung up near Palm Beach and was now Dayuma's home village. Rachel was overjoyed when she learned that Wycliffe/SIL had given her permission to return to the Waorani and live with Dayuma at Tonampade. She had just been diagnosed with cancer and had been given a limited amount of time to live. Whatever time was left, she wanted to spend it among her adopted family.

By November 1994 Rachel's health had failed, and Rachel allowed herself to be airlifted to Quito, where her friends Jim and Sharon Smith offered to take care of her. Rachel knew that she would never return to the jungle again, and she spent much of her days reliving the special times she had spent with the Waorani. She thought about when she had first heard of Dayuma, and when she heard that other Waoranis had walked out of the jungle. She recalled Dayuma's first halting prayer and the day Kimo told her they had talked God's Carvings while she had been away. Then she remembered back to when she was eighteen years old on the ocean liner and recalled the vision she had seen of naked jungle people beckoning to her to come and tell them the Good News. That vision had come true, and Rachel was sure that she had lived the life God intended for her to live.

On November 11, 1994, feeling weak but purposeful, Rachel turned to Jim and Sharon and said, "Well, I guess I'd better go to heaven so you can get back to work." Then she started to pray, alternating between Spanish and Waorani. Soon she squeezed Sharon's hand and was gone.

Rachel's nephew Steve flew from Florida to Quito to arrange a funeral service there. When the service was over, Rachel's body was taken on one last flight over her beloved jungle to Tonampade. A hundred Waorani gathered on the landing strip to welcome Nimu home. Dayuma and Dawa broke into loud sobs as the plane touched down, and soon the others did also.

The Waoranis carried Rachel's coffin to the church and held their own funeral service, after which Rachel was to be buried beside the church, a short distance from her brother Nate's gravesite.

At the funeral service, Minkayi spoke last. "She called us her brothers. She told us how to believe. Now she is in heaven. Happy and laughing, she is in heaven. Only those who believe go to heaven."

Komi, Dayuma's husband, nodded and added, "God is building a house for all of us, and that's where we'll see Nimu again."

Dawa joined in. "Nimu's brother came, and killing him, we did not do well. Nimu came, and believing, we did well."

Bibliography

Elliot, Elisabeth. *Through Gates of Splendor*. Wheaton, Ill.: Tyndale House Publishers, 1956.

Hefley, James and Marti. *Unstilled Voices*. Chappaqua, NY.: Christian Herald Books, 1981.

Hitt, Russell T. *Jungle Pilot*. Grand Rapids: Discovery House Publishers, 1997.

Kingsland, Rosemary. *A Saint Among Savages*. London: Collins, 1980.

Wallis, Ethel Emily. *Dayuma: Life Under Waorani Spears*. Seattle: YWAM Publishing, 1996.

About the Authors

Janet and Geoff Benge are a husband and wife writing team with more than thirty years of writing experience. Janet is a former elementary school teacher. Geoff holds a degree in history. Originally from New Zealand, the Benges spent ten years serving with Youth With A Mission. They have two daughters, Laura and Shannon, and an adopted son, Lito. They make their home in the Orlando, Florida, area.